My … our support

Kate Anolue

THE AUTOBIOGRAPHY

A good head and a good heart are
always a formidable combination.

- Nelson Mandela

Kate Anolue

THE AUTOBIOGRAPHY

Kate Anolue

(Adajelumba Tulugo1 of Nanka)

http://www.KateAnolue.com

London, UK

Email: Kate@KateAnolue.com

ISBN: 978-1-64570-007-4

Dedication

This book is dedicated to my late parents; Chief Fidelis Ezeobuoha Ezeasor *(Okwuolisa)* & Princess Veronica Egbeichi Ezeasor nee Ezeugwa (*Okwesilieze Umuagbala*), and my late husband Ifeanyichukwu Festus Anolue.

One who is too insistent on his own views, finds few to agree with him.

-Lao Tzu

Acknowledgements

My life cannot be what it is today without the love and care of my late father Chief Fidelis Ezeobuoha Ezeasor *(Okwuolisa)* who believed in gender equality and gave me the opportunity to have a full education as he did for his five sons. This was despite his friends telling him it was a waste of money to educate a girl child. *Papa Anyi* (our father) as I call him, you made me who I am today *Daalu* (Thank you), and I miss you dearly.

My late mother *Mama Anyi* (our mother) as we always call her, Princess Veronica Egbeichi Ezeasor (*Okwesilieze Umuagbala*), who defied everything and breastfed me for four good years, transferring all of her good qualities like amazingly good health, humility, leadership skills, strength and stamina. My mother spoke with her eyes and actions rather than her voice. This and so much more, I learnt from her. I have never seen or heard my mother argue or quarrel with other women, which gained her a lot of respect. I have been able to emulate some of my mother's qualities, and they have helped me in coping with some types of people who I have come across, especially women. "*Mama Anyi, anam ekene gi. Daalu, Na nudo*" "(Our mother, I am greeting you, thank you for your love, go in peace).

I thank my late husband Ifeanyichukwu Festus Anolue, who kept his promise to my father by allowing me to continue my education. He supported me throughout my Nursing and Midwifery training. I thank him for all his help. He was a husband, father, soul mate, lover and friend. You are just one in a million.

I thank all of my siblings for the love, support and respect they showered on me. It is difficult to list them individually; as they all played significant roles in my life. They also manage my interests in Nigeria. They have always been there for my children, been role models for my two sons and supported Amaechi, my first son when he was studying at the Federal College, Enugu. They were my bodyguards.

I thank all of my children. You were my rock all the way; sometimes you could be a pain, but inwardly I am so happy that you all came into my life. Single parenting is not easy, but seeing how they turned out; I believe I did a good job. You understood me just like I did my mother who spoke with her eyes rather than voice, and I love you all.

My appreciations also go to the traditional ruler of Nanka, HRH Godwin Ezekunyie Ezeilo Ezeadusionu *(Obu*Nanka) and his Cabinet and Chiefs, including Chief Poly Emenike, (*Odenigbo* Nanka), Chief Ebere Nwosu, (*Ezeudo* Nanka), Chief Peter Chinedu, (*Onwa* Nanka), Chief Kofi Obijiofor (*Ajie* Nanka). Chief Damian Okeke (*Ogene* Nanka). Chief Okwudili Ezenwankwo (*Ewepudike* Nanka) ; Chairman Ohaneze Anambra State BranchMember-Elect Orumba North & South Federal Constituency House of Representatives. Nigeria, among many other Chiefs and Cabinet members that space would not allow me to mention by name here. Special thanks to President General of the Ohanaeze Ndigbo, Chief Nnia Nwodo and Chief Mrs Bianca Ojukwu for your support and encouragement to Ndigbo.

I thank all my friends who were there for me at my point of need; Cecilia Okeke and her family who looked after Amaechi during his time at Federal College, Enugu. You were his second family who supported and shaped his future. I thank you and I'm very grateful. Cecilia Eke, who

I met at North Middlesex maternity over forty years ago; you took me as your sister and made sure that I did not work too hard in the Labour ward, especially while I was pregnant. You and your husband had to be Chukwuma's godparents. I am grateful to Mr & Mrs Agbasonu, family friends of my husband; your friendship with my late husband was extended to me while I was still in Nigeria. You helped me to settle easily in the UK, especially sourcing names of hospitals I should apply to for my Nursing career.

I thank Mrs Bernadette Osuagwu and her family for their support at the time I needed it the most. You allowed your teenage daughter, Dorothy to spend the night whenever I needed her to (on days when I was on call). My special thanks to Dorothy, your help was irreplaceable. I was able to maintain a full-time job because I know you were there and available whenever I needed you. Thank you so much.

My dear Jenny Chika Okafor; we met over thirty years ago through unique circumstances. We have remained close to one another and you have been inspirational to many things in my life especially encouraging me in writing this book. You are a great woman with outstanding intelligence; you have many ideas, you are not selfish, and you share even the million-dollar winning ideas with all. Always ready to share your thoughts. I thank you and appreciate you.

I thank Victoria Akudike for her unconditional support in many ways especially travelling to Nigeria with me on both occasions of my parents passing on. You trusted me so much that you made me godparent to both of your children. I haven't done much for them, yet I only have to sneeze and my goddaughter, Ify will quickly come to look after me, shopping and cooking with your support. I am blessed.

I thank you, Jackie Fanning and Nneka Keazor. Since you both came into my life, I gained two more daughters. I was physically involved in the birth of your children; hence I see them as my grandchildren. You both enriched my life in many ways, hence my youthful attitude to life and perhaps also, my ways of thinking.

Ken and Joe Ife; wow, super family! You came into my life when I needed that extended family support and trust where my children could grow with a father figure role model around them. I remember all those New Year's Eve partying till dawn and Ken's breakfast spread. I really miss all that. It's a pity we cannot rewind the clock; it was a great time filled with fun. I thank and appreciate you both.

Helen Ogbu, my special friend. We met by chance over thirty years ago in labour ward, North Middlesex University hospital where I looked after you. I vividly remember the expression on your face when I spoke in the Igbo language to you. You were overjoyed. You put your trust and confidence in me to care for you and from that brief moment, we built a nurse-patient relationship. When you were discharged from the hospital, I declined to give you my phone number. Despite that, you were still able to obtain it. From where? I do not know, but you meant well. We became family and you introduced me to your extended family.

To all my godchildren, Ify, Kenny, the twins (Danny and Sammy), Chisom, Araba, Connor, Rose, Anne, Joanna, Laura and many more, I love you all. Please forgive me if I have not been in your life as I should.

I want to thank the Leader of Enfield Council Nesil Caliskan, the Chief Executive Ian Davies, and Law & Governance Jeremy Chambers for believing in me and giving me the opportunity to realise my dream of introducing the Young Mayor for the first time in Enfield Council. I will forever be grateful.

I thank my special childhood friend since age five, Mrs Mercellina (Mercy) Onyebuchi. We may live thousands of miles away from each other, but we are always together and support one another during times of joy and sadness. Thanks to modern technology that made it possible for us to speak on the phone or WhatsApp anytime. We formed a unique friendship of over sixty years, which extended to both families. Childhood friendship is one of the most beautiful memories that can never be replaced. Friends are the family we choose for ourselves.

I would not have completed my Law degree without the unconditional support from my colleague and special friend for over forty years Blossom Davidson. You were always on standby on my lecture days and ready to take over from me when I am running past my duty hours in the maternity ward at North Middlesex University Hospital Edmonton. You always made sure that I was not late or missed my lectures. You were like my lost sister from a different world. We supported one another in our profession and showed sincere appreciation of each other's progress and promotion. You were not like most of the women I met on my journey. You encouraged me and you were happy with my educational development. Great atmosphere, hence I spent all my working life at North Middlesex hospital. I like to take the opportunity here to pay tribute to my very good friend and colleague, Carmen Steel who we lost to cancer last year. May her soul rest in perfect peace. Amen. Some of the friends I mentioned in this book have lost their spouses. May their souls rest in peace. Amen.

I wish to thank all the midwives, staff and doctors who helped to lift me up when I returned to work after my husband passed away. You were all great. I'm grateful to Mrs Faruqi, my Community Nursing Officer where ever you are now. Your help and support allowed me to settle back quickly into work. You adjusted the rota to suit my children and me, making it easy for me to arrange help when needed; you are a gem!

I sincerely thank so many organisations and groups who have given me the honour either to be the patron of their organisation, Leader or even find me worthy to seek my advice and opinion at times; Council of Igbo Leaders, Ohanaeze Ndigbo, Adaure Igbo Women, Prestigious Ada Nanka, Elect Ladies of Substance, Igbo Cultural Support Network (ICSN). Nigerian Women in Diaspora Leadership Forum (NWIDLF), Central Association of Nigerians in the UK (CANUK), UK Nollywood Producers Guild, St. Edmunds Nigerian Community, Igbo Catholic Community, Nigerian Catholic Christian Women Organisation (NCCWO). I thank the leaders and elders in the Nigerian communities I have come across in many different ways, I admire you all.

Special thanks to Yetunde Adeshile, who has worked so hard with me in preparing my conferences, especially the artwork and giving up your time to support me in many ways, wow, I am blessed. June Douglas, you are just amazing. Your support is incredible; I thank God for knowing you.

Christine Adamu, my dance partner, thank you so much for the last ten years; you have been there for me, and we have supported each other, I am grateful. I am glad I have all you young people around me; you give me the push and infuse me with enormous energy. I am not complaining. Getty, you are always there for me, and I thank you so much.

Sir & Lady Iwu, you are a great family; out of the blue, my daughters wanted you in their lives. Thank you for accepting them. I have no doubt that whatever they seek from your Christian practice, they will get. Thank you for being there for them and your goddaughter Kamsiyochukwu. It gives me great joy to know you are there for them.

Geraldine Chioma Obi-Nwagwu (*Ugonwanyi*) and MargaretChukwudi (*Ugogbe njiafuzo*). I'm so happy to know both of you. You have a friendship that I admire. You care for each other and that is what matters. Keep up the good work, and I love you both.

I thank you Fr. Emmanuel Ogunnaike, the Parish Priest of St. Edmunds for your support in many ways especially in my mayoral year "2012/2013". You were always there with open hands, advice and listening ears. I thank all the Reverend Fathers and the Religious leaders whom I have met on my journey especially Reverend Sister Vitalis Chigbu, your advice, and support is immeasurable.

Ayo Akinfe, how can I forget you, you are always there for me; always sorting out my problems even when I call from Nigeria. I am so happy to know you, and I thank you very much.

Special thanks to Dr Dayo Olomu, who advised me to write my story, little did he know that I was already doing so. I began writing this book over three years ago, but your encouragement and advice that I should write my story helped me conclude that I was on the right path. I don't like blowing my own trumpet; hence I kept quiet. I thank you for your empowering words. I always admire you.

There are many others but this book cannot accommodate all. I am sorry if I have not mentioned you. I would like you to know that I love you, I appreciate you and, I am grateful for having you in life.

My special appreciation goes to my book consultant Felicity Okolo and her team for making sure this book is as perfect as I want it to be. Felicity Okolo can be contacted by email: **Felicity.Okolo@gmail.com**

"It's what you practice in private that you will be rewarded for in public."

– Tony Robbins

Contents

Prologue

In the Mighty name of Jesus! I recall what the bible said about living to SEVENTY YEARS.

Yesooooo!!! In Psalm 90:10 –It says, "The years of your life are seventy, or even by reason of strength eighty, yet their span is but toil and trouble, but they are soon gone, and we fly away".

In Jeremiah 29:10 – "For thus says the Lord" *When seventy years are completed for Babylon, I will visit you, and I will fulfil to you my promise and bring you back to this place."*

But the Lord wasn't promising that every person would live to be seventy or eighty; however, I believe the psalmist is just describing our normal human experience. For even the best years of our lives are filled with pain and trouble. Our time is in God's hand, and for some, their journey on earth is even much shorter. We all have a reason why God created us, and once you have completed your assignment, you are recalled. I see life as just a market place, where people come to shop and trade at different times, and when you are done shopping, you go home. Even when you are going back to the same house, one person always steps in first before the other.

Within the monarchies, the seventieth anniversary is celebrated as a Platinum Jubilee. Thus, recognising the importance, the Bible has emphasised on reaching seventy years in our life. This is followed by the special hundredth year which is the centenary celebration. As we know only a few people reach this milestone, and the Queen of England does not miss sending a birthday card to any of her subjects who attain a hundred years in this beautiful world.

As for Kate Anolue or rather Aunty Kate, as I prefer to be called by most people, I want to celebrate every day of my entire life, and of course, I also believe that seventy years marks a special stage in my life."Every birthday is a gift. Every day is a gift." Aretha Franklin 1942-2018.

Life is what you make it, a free and democratic world. As adults, it is left to us what we want to make of the world and the life in it. I believe as the saying goes "as you make your bed, so must you lie in it." Growing old gracefully does not emerge overnight, it is a gradual process. Our body is sacred and so must be treated with respect. Humility is an acquired wealth to all humans, but only a few make the most of it. We let our selfishness; envious nature and pride overshadow the blessings that God has bestowed upon us. With that attitude, we pull apart the gift of ageing gracefully which the Almighty in His infinite goodness gave to us. Health is essential to us all and as we get older, it becomes even more important; hence, we will do anything naturally possible to maintain good health from cradle to grave. There is clear evidence that leisure and culture when linked with life and social skills, improve quality of life.

This might sound like a lecture, but it is in my nature to say and do the right thing. I will continue by saying that a good diet alone will not suffice; it must be balanced with leisure activities like yoga, Pilates, swimming, dancing, gardening, brisk walking and so many more. These also increases your social network, enhance your mood, boost your confidence, self-esteem, and the total wellbeing of your mind and body. Exercise will help to prevent and manage a wide range of health problems including stroke, high blood pressure, and metabolic syndrome, type two diabetes, depression, a number of types of cancer, arthritis and falls and control weight gain.

Everyone benefits from exercise regardless of age, gender or physical activity. Most people think you must devote some special time for exercise, No!!! You don't have to. All you need is to be more active throughout your day. Use the stairs instead of the elevator or lift. Increase your household chores, do things yourself at times instead of always engaging house help. Consistency is the keyword. You don't have to wait and go with someone or your friend, you can make friends at the gym, gardening group, leisure centres, or anywhere you choose to do your exercise. These friends remain for that purpose. I have got my swim friends, three of us. Occasionally we go out for lunch or dinner, and that is where good and lasting friendships start, especially since we share the same interest. Waiting for someone to go with draws you back and you may never achieve your aim.

Why do I insist on people adding the prefix "aunty" to my name? I would like to take you back to the picture I took with my mother in June 2016, (my Facebook profile photo) that was when she was ninety years and four months old. She appeared calm, her face was clear of wrinkles and no sign of stress, her skin was beautiful, and she was very ambulant. That picture did not reflect her age.

Well, I thank God that I inherited that wonderful youthful gene. I have lots of male and female friends who are ten to twenty years younger than me, but I just have a natural way of fitting in. Hence, it was necessary for me to show that there was a boundary that cannot be crossed. Age is a number, and I believe that if you feel hundred, you will definitely behave like you were hundred, and if you feel twenty, you will also behave likewise. I am young at heart and I love myself. It is the best attitude to life, especially when people want to run you down out of jealousy or their own inferiority complex. I have come across women who manipulate their fellow women just for their own selfish conquest.

Unfortunately, believe it or not, there are still people who are followers and can easily lead too. You could be sitting in your house and in the blink of an eye, you have made many enemies through lies and gossip. I had always believed that gossips were for when we were growing, but as parents, we would be more mature and wiser. As we get older, we acquire generations of experience of how people should behave.

It is sad that some women who are supposed to be parents are still running around the community, causing havoc as they seek to be noticed. It makes me wonder what example they show and teach to their children. But in life, you must trust and believe in yourself. Be disciplined, determined and never give up. Manipulators operate in different patterns. First of all, they manufacture lies, and because they are prolific liars with sweet but acid tongues, you can be easily forced to believe what you hear. Naturally, if you have been told that someone said something negative about you, they immediately become your enemy, and a barrier automatically creates itself for you. The saying "silence is the best answer to a f…" because responding is giving them the platform that will level you with them. There is an Igbo saying, "*mmadu nabo adi aho ara na ofumgbe*" meaning "two people cannot be mad at the same time". If you listen to all negative comments about yourself, you are then missing the opportunity of concentration, which might be the only time and window God has allocated for you to think and make the most of yourself. No matter how good you are, there are still millions of enemies out there for you. My rule is, keep them at arm's length and ignore them at all times. Most important, is to move on and don't look back.

For in Proverbs 13:3, it says "*Whoever guards his mouth preserves his life; he who opens wide his lips comes to ruin.*"

In Proverb 10:14 it says, "*The wise store up knowledge, but the mouth of the fool invites destruction*".

Life isn't about finding yourself. Life is about creating yourself.

- George Barnard Shaw

Chapter One

IT'S MY STORY

Life they say is a journey and mine is a sweet and sour one, but I have embraced it with thanks and gratitude to the Almighty who has blessed me with wonderful good health, and I have little to nothing to complain about. When I look at myself in the mirror, I always say "Yes girl, keep it up". I am very conscious about my body and that is because I love clothes and dressing up, and it must fit well. My designer, who also happens to be my cousin, keeps me right on top of the latest styles. She is an amazing, talented fashion guru. I don't need to tell her what style I want, she always goes for the best for me. I love dancing and never miss the opportunity to shake my tired bones when good music is playing. "If music be the food of love, play on, Give me excess of it; that surfeiting, The appetite may sicken, and so die" from Shakespeare's Twelfth night, 1602. Music plays an important part in Shakespeare's plays and is often used to carry the plot.

It all started from my place of birth in Jos, Plateau State, Northern Nigeria. I was born to Igbo parents *Ichie* and *Lolo* Ezeasor, both from Nanka in Orumba North Local Government Area (L.G.A) of Anambra State. I have six siblings; a sister and five brothers. All six of us were born in the North, and the baby of the family was born in Eastern Nigeria as it was then called. My younger sister was only a few months old when we had to move back to the East due to the civil war. Just to satisfy the curious question or thought brewing in your mind at this time, yes, I still understand Hausa, the popular language spoken in Northern Nigeria and I still speak it, but it is not very fluent as it used to be. It's amazing how quickly one can forget if you are out of touch and have no way of practising. It is always said that practice makes perfect. It is a language I was privileged to learn, and I am eager to re-learn.

My mother, late Princess Veronica Egbeichi Ezeasor was born into the Great Ezeugwa Royal family of Ifite Nanka in Orumba North L.G.A of Anambra State in 1926. She was the fourth of eight children of the late Ekemezie Ezeugwa (*Osuofia, Aka OseAdinma Na Anya*) and late Martha Ifekanma Ezeugwa (*ChukwuNweOlu).* She had one younger sister Theresa, who is now the only surviving sibling. She got married at the matured age of twenty-one to late *Ichie* Fidelis Ezeobuoha Ezeasor (*Okwuolisa*), and they moved to Jos, Plateau State, where they lived happily until the civil war broke out.

My mother was an intelligent woman, but as it was in those days, girls did not have the opportunity of going to school. But I could tell if she had the slightest window to education, she would have excelled and likewise my dad. My father, other than Primary school, had no further education. Both of them however believed in education and made sure that all seven of their children had a good education without gender discrimination.

As a devout Catholic, "Mama Anyi" as we always called our mother, was very active in many religious groups and was honoured with many titles which include *Okwesilieze Umuagbala,Nne Di Ugwu, Ada Bu Ugwu, Igbo AkuEnyi* and many more. She lived up to the standards of purity expected of a devout Christian.

What a special mother she was; a successful trader and a strong, independent woman. She never had any live-in helper to assist with household chores, and in bringing up her large family. She brought up her children especially the girls to be independent, strong and will-powered. She gave me everything, starting from psychological resilience, calm in any situation, strength, energy, will power, above all good health and youthfulness. All these I acquired through what you could never guess; breastfeeding me until the age of four. I was shocked when she revealed that to me, and only because she found out that I breastfed my first child for one year which she told me off for..

I believe she literally transferred all the qualities I needed to cope in life, especially having encountered early widowhood too, as if she already knew what my future held. I thank God that I had the opportunity to say THANK YOU to her in various ways, but it was never enough. The word "Cathy" will continue to ring in my ears because that was my mother's last word to me the day I called her, and she could not say much except to call my name as she always did. This was less than ten days before she answered God's call.

When my mother passed away on the 27th of July 2017, I was already eighteen months into writing this book. I thank the Almighty above that she lived a fulfilled and fruitful life to see her seven children grow into fathers and mothers; blessing her with many grand and great-grandchildren.

My father came from a polygamous home where his father had two wives. Polygamy was highly practised by people from the Eastern region at that time but not so much these days. My father was one of nine children from his mother; there were four boys and five girls, and my father was the baby of the family and from his mother's side as well. He was very much loved and spoilt by his siblings, and parents.

My father was a businessman. He engaged in trading and motor transport. He travelled extensively within Nigeria and its neighbouring countries until the civil war broke out. Before he married my mother, he lived in a place called Utonkon in the Tiv area of Benue State, North Central Zone of Nigeria. After they got married, they travelled and lived in Jos, Plateau State in the Northern part of Nigeria. This was where they lived all their married life until the civil war broke in 1966 and they had to move back to the East hurriedly.

My youngest brother was born in the East, the same year that I had my first daughter, but my daughter is older than him. My daughter was born in February while my youngest brother was born in August of the same year. Other than that, six of us were born in the North.

I am the eldest of seven children, and I think it was really nice, but also it carries a lot of responsibilities. I think and believe that I was really carved out to be a leader. Not because I was the first child, because some first children in the family may not be leaders.

My mother usually left me in charge of all my siblings, and it was quite easy to manage them and they all respected and listened to me, and still do. I think it's because of the way I communicated with them. I was never a bossy sister, but I was firm. I was like a leader. I led them as though I knew what I was doing and if they paid attention, things would work out fine. They trusted my judgment, and for some reason, I have always been fortunate. If I ask them to do something because it is the right thing to do, it always turns out to be the right thing. So, I never had any problems with them. Most siblings fight, but amazingly we never fought. There was nothing like fighting in my family amongst us siblings while we were growing up.

My parents were two wonderful people and my mum was one of the most humble and conservative woman I have ever met. Despite her family background, she was quiet and did not like showing off, even when her children were progressive in their chosen careers. I learnt all about humility and no pride from my late mother. She had successful children and yet she did not display it with pride or in a disrespectful manner to other women or family. Due to this attitude, she gained respect from all quarters. She had peace of mind at all times; there was no fear or concern for herself or her children. She remained the leader of all the women in our village, the Christian Mothers and a life member of the Catholic Women Organisation till her last day in the world. May her soul rest in peace. Amen.

My mother, *mama anyi* loved the home and was an excellent housewife. Although she had a large family, she was hardworking and coped very well with no extra live-in help. I like to call my mother a businesswoman because she sold food items, some wholesale and some retail. I liked it because I would always come home quickly from school to take over from her at the stall. This is one thing that I really enjoyed. You know how most children play on their way from school? I didn't have the time. I quickly went to my mother's stall so she could go to her weekday church activities like Legion of Mary, St Theresa, Our Lady of Lourdes meetings and all that. At times when I know she had no religious meeting, I would play a lot before coming home from school, climbing mango trees in search of ripe mango fruit. I was a real tomboy; I often wanted to show boys I could equally climb mango trees. Although my school was girls only, we do meet up with the boys on the way home. There was no misbehaviour or rowdiness though, we had the reputation of our school to protect by showing good behaviour on our way home.

Back in Nigeria, schools finish at 1pm whereas it ends at 3.15pm in the UK, and it was usually a long distance from home. We trekked for about an hour but we didn't feel it. Sometimes it could mean trekking barefooted, but we enjoyed it because we were among other children and there was no envy amongst us. As soon as I got home, I would go to take over the stall from my mother. When we got home in the evenings, after our meal, I would start on my homework.

On Saturdays, my mother would let me go to her market stall and spend about four good hours before she comes to take over. And by this time, I would have made a lot of sales. I was very young; I think I was between eight to ten years and very clever when it came to things like that. I always wanted to run business, and I was usually lucky as I had a lot of customers. One might think that a child my age would feel tired, but I never was.. I suppose this was where I built up the stamina that is helping me even now as an adult because I have always been a busy person. . I also like to credit myself for my ability to multi-task. So, you can see how busy I have been all my life.

I do not think or feel that I missed out on childhood because of my busy schedule. Besides, we had Sundays. And also, I did what I had to do because I wanted to, not just because my mother wanted me to. I just wanted to come home from school and be a part of it. I didn't feel like it was my obligation as the first child to help out with making money and to relieve my mother. The only time I felt like it was my obligation to make sure things were going alright was during the civil war.

During the civil war, I was about thirteen years old. There was a lot of hunger and malnutrition, and because I was very close to and really loved my siblings, I hated that any of my siblings had to experience that. So, I felt like I had to do something to help my parents. Aha, you see! It was during the civil war that all those skills I acquired, like helping my mum in the stall manifested and really helped me. My cousins and I did a lot of things to help earn money for the family. In the evenings, we make soups like *egusi, ogbono* or *okra*. I was an expert in *ogbono* and *okra* soup. We would get up at midnight and carry the pot of soup on our heads and trek for three to four good hours to arrive at our destination town at about 5am in the morning. In that town called Awa there were a lot of fresh foodstuffs. The inhabitants of the town were farmers and there were a lot of lorries transporting people and traders from places like Onitsha, Awka, Igboukwu, Awgbu and other far away towns. They all arrived very early to buy fresh vegetables and foodstuff at wholesale prices, and to get back to other towns where the goods would be retailed and some wholesaled.

All the traders must have departed at night to arrive in the morning. Before they arrive, we were already there. We would have had our firewood stove running, making *eba* (cassava fu-fu) and selling with the soup we brought (in Nigerian slang, it is called "*mama put*"). My soup was always very nice, so between 10am and 11am, I was usually sold out. Once your soup is finished, that was it for the day. My customers would always ask, "Why is it that your soup always finishes quickly?"

I make friends everywhere, and I have some good friends. There was a lady then, who would always come to my stall to have her breakfast – fufu and my lovely soup. In time we become good friends. One day she said to me, "Why don't you just get your ingredients and come to spend the night in my house, so that first thing in the morning you can start cooking and then you can cook much more."

Typically, when we cooked at my place, we only cooked what we could carry. So, I decided to take the lady's offer. I told my cousins, and they asked me to ask if it was okay for all three of us to spend the night at her place. She said, "Yes of course!" Back home in those days, all you need to sleep on is a clean floor and a nice mat. She made room for us, and we got our mats. We got to her place at about 11pm, so we could get about four hours of sleep. First thing in the morning, we started cooking.

At the lady's place, I made a massive pot of okra soup. On the first day, we sold and sold, and I made so much money that I thought, wow! Because I had enough soup, I was able to keep selling until the lorry drivers were getting back on the road. The market was like a wholesaler's market where they came to buy in bulk. I sold until they finished buying. And that was how we carried on once a week in *Afo-Awa*. I also made a lot of profit from the roasted peanuts I sold on *Afor* days; that was if my younger sister did not eat up all of my profit. During the war, a lot of families went through malnutrition and starvation. This was so because most of the time, there was only carbohydrates and no meat or proteins and things like that. In as much as we were a large family, we never suffered that. This was because my father farmed, my mother engaged in petty trading, and I was busy doing "mama put" and also frying my *akara* (bean cake) and roasting peanuts.

Sometimes, we went to the other inner towns that produced rice. We would buy rice from there and sell it at another market where we would make a lot of profit. I did not sell the rice in *AforUdoNanka,* only my *akara* and peanuts because there were too many people selling rice. We also bought other little foodstuff materials so that even when we did not make any profit, we could use whatever was left for our own use.

In Igbo land, they are four market days- *Nkwo, Eke, Oye, Afor* - and I trekked for miles with my cousins to different towns each day according to the market day to buy and sell. Each town had its own market day and what they specialised in. At Nkwo-Igbo we bought bulk vegetables such as *Ugu* and sold wholesale in our hometown. We used to make good profit. Sometimes, when we did not make profit, we would at least breakeven and still have vegetables left over to use at home.

When it was my town's market day, I always made *akara.* Our market day is *Afor,* and the market square is called *AforUdoNanka.* On that *Afor* day, I would fry *akara* or roast peanuts or groundnuts as is popularly known in Nigeria. I did have a lot of fun. My peanuts were always very tasty. After roasting and selling the peanuts, I would buy all the necessary food items needed for a balanced diet for our large family. I was the little mother, and sometimes I had enough spare money to buy a football for my brothers. In those days, we lived like refugees in the communal Ezeasor compound. My father having spent all those years in Northern Nigeria had no building he could call his. .We had two rooms; one room that all of the children slept in, and the second was a communal room to chill out and receive visitors. Although we were in our hometown, we were still refugees as we left all our property behind in Jos. It was very hard for my parents and seven children to adjust and "eat from plate to mouth", and all the while, the civil war was getting intense. Our solace was that we were in our town as there were other displaced people who came to settle in our town (Nanka) and had to abandon their home and property. One advantage of this period of instability was that I was able to meet and know a lot of my cousins, relations, and other family members especially my mother's siblings and their families. However, I still noticed that we were the outsiders. I had to be strong to make sure that I helped my parents in taking care of my siblings. With all these, I still did not allow my family duties to overtake my social life. I joined the student union in my town Nanka and was able to play active parts in the activities of the youths as much as I could.

My younger sister whom I love very much always accompanied me everywhere I went. I remembered looking for her in the house one day, but I could not find her. She was only about two or three years old at the time. She was born in the year that the civil war broke out (1966). So, I kept calling out for her; "*Nneka, Nnekamuo, NneNne.*" But she did not answer. We could not find her anywhere. I know what had happened and for some reason, my curiosity took over me. I bent and saw her hiding under the bed eating up the peanut that I was going to sell. I believe she was eating the peanuts that were supposed to be for my business. Till this day, I still remember it. My mother also remembered it too. It was a very fond memory that makes me smile and laugh whenever I remember.

She didn't know what she was doing or that she was going to cost me my profit. All she knew was she was enjoying her nuts. I didn't tell her off because I loved her so much. The rest of my siblings are; Arinze who came after me, then Edozie, Amaechi, Chukwud*i* then Louisa or Nneka and finally, the baby of the family Ifeanyi or Polycarp. I call my only sister "Louie-Louie" or "Louie-Nne" even till now.

When my mother had my brother Arinze, she then had the next child who was also a boy, and the next two were also boys. When she had the fourth consecutive boy, "no, no, no," I thought to myself. This was wrong and unfair, "how could she keep having all these boys?" I refused to go to visit her in the hospital. I said because all she kept doing was having all these "stupid" boys. I said that she did not like me and that was the reason why she refused to give me a sister. So, when someone asked me "I heard your mother had a baby, what did she have?" I answered rhetorically, "Oh well, what else would she have?" I could not believe I had said: "The same thing that she's been having is all she had." I think I was about ten years or slightly over, and I meant every comment I made. But then it showed how ignorant we were in those days. There was nothing called sex education, so no idea of who or what was responsible for making a girl or boy baby. My mum's sex education to me when I left home for teachers' training college, Akwanga was to be a good girl and come my next holiday, she would buy me a nice suitcase. I never understood what she meant, because as far as I was concerned, I was a good girl. It took many years before I learnt what she meant was to keep away from boys. I cannot even remember how we handled my menarche. Everything was like a sign language, but I could always read my mother's lips.

As soon as we came back from the North, we started school straight away. I joined Loretta Adazi Teacher's Training College and managed to study for one year before the full outbreak of the war. We only studied for maybe two months before the war became intensive and everyone started running away. However, we were lucky because our town was further in so we did not have to move. Nanka was one of the towns that were not affected by the war. In fact, we were taking in refugees. It had its disadvantage. The disadvantage was that Nanka had big erosions that still plague the town till this day.

It was only during the war that I felt like it was my obligation to support my parents in taking care of my siblings financially. And for some reason, it felt like I was already armed for this responsibility. The skills I picked up from joining my mother at the market stall after school or on Saturdays; going to run the market for her before she came to take over, did serve us tremendously. Now, looking at war-torn countries, I feel sympathy for the children caught up in these wars; their experience is worst. They are exploited sexually, emotionally and physically abused. Not all human beings retain their humanity in these periods. There is no doubt that a lot of families and children suffered and had terrible experiences during the Nigerian Civil war, but I am writing about myself and my experience.

There were no sibling rivalries amongst my siblings and myself, or else I do not know how it would have affected us during the war. With regards to homework, I was not affected because I was very bright. I either came first or second in my class. Whenever I came second, I was not usually happy. Back in those days in Nigeria, the teachers always made use of the intelligent ones. They always sent us on errands knowing that we will catch up quickly. So, we were basically the teacher's pets.

My most memorable experiences from childhood up till the age of ten were being a kind of leader, being in charge of my siblings and also being able to help my parents. It felt like I was the younger mummy. And funny enough, I still remember these things. My siblings knew they could rely on me and they trusted me. It was like being in charge but also at the same time not being bossy or undermining them. I have the greatest respect for my siblings up till now. Regardless of the closeness between siblings, once they start getting married, certain things are bound to change. New wives wanted to build their own home, and the men began to listen more to their wives as they try to build their own families. These changes are very obvious when I am visiting Nigeria. Usually, all my four brothers would come for me at the airport. They were like my bodyguards and sometimes they were accompanied by our cousins. It was always a special moment for me. These days, it is usually one or two brothers, and at times, my sisters-in-law also come to receive me at the airport.

Hardships often prepare ordinary people for an extraordinary destiny.

– C.S. Lewis

Chapter Two

MY SCHOOL YEARS

With regards to friends, my school years were amazing and beautiful; we had healthy competitions in the classroom and on the school grounds. Nothing breaks a friendship, not even when you or your friends excel better. School-wise, when it came to sports, I was very good at netball. I loved to play netball, and I represented my school in netball competitions. I was the captain and also the goal shooter. This was where I found my friends; I believed in those who shared the same interests as me, which limited the number of sincere friends I had then.

Although I loved sports and running, I was not very good at it either. My siblings still make jokes about my heavy feet. But when it comes to netball, yes! That was where I shone! I knew that I was good at it and I enjoyed it. We also went on netball tournaments, where I enjoyed to turn up in style. We looked forward to the tournaments as they were one of the main avenues of meeting and making friends from other schools.

For me, school years were such glorious moments as there was nothing like bullying. As far as we were concerned, life was tied together in beautiful knots and untied stage by stage as we grew up. Life is nothing and absolutely nothing. I have remained in communication with many of my friends since I came to the UK; some in the diaspora and some in Nigeria.

In the UK, I soon found out how difficult it was to make and keep friends. I did not experience much difficulty, however. I soon made friends within my nursing profession and a few more from the church. Interestingly, I was given some lectures about making friends within our community. It did not really bother me, but I just became slightly cautious when making friends at that stage of my life. I was now a mother and extremely family focused, so I wanted to integrate with other parents for my benefit and for those of my children.

While I was growing up, on weekends, we would go on outings with our mum and other family members. All the children play and socialise together, and I have done the same with my children here in London. There were a lot of community engagements and parties, but these were usually in the afternoons and not evenings as in London. Sometimes on Sundays, after eating that lovely rice and stew or *joloff* rice (specially cooked every Sunday in almost all households) after church, we would go on outings to the Zoo and Theme Parks. Surprisingly, there were Theme Parks in Northern Nigeria in those days like we have in London. I learnt a lot from my mother who always took my siblings and me to church events and community outings practically every weekend. I was prepared for motherhood and childcare at a very early age. I learnt a lot about community and women empowerment through my mother's activities in the church and a lot of women group meetings that I accompanied her to. I cannot in any way think my mother ever overworked me, as I also had a lot of opportunities to be with my friends; especially my childhood friend Mercellina whom I call Mercy or Lina, whom I met on the day our parents brought us to school for the first time. We have remained friends ever since and that has been over sixty-five years now. Childhood friendships are one of the most beautiful memories that can never be replaced. I have two other great friends whom I met in my nursing profession. This has been over forty years, and all our children grew together. These were solid friendships; "FRIENDS ARE THE FAMILY WE CHOOSE FOR OURSELVES."

Regrettably these days, friendships have turned into competitions; instead of being inspired and empowered by those you call friends, you begin to question God about why those kinds of friends came into your life in the first place.

Social media has not helped either. I believe it has created many kinds of people:

1. Those who think before talking.
2. Those who don't think while there are talking, and finally,
3. Those who think they are thinking while they are talking, but are not really thinking.

A bit confusing? Not really. We are what we are, for what has happened in our life now, because we allowed digital devices to organise our life.

For Psalm 34:13; says "Keep your tongue from evil and your lips from deceitful speech."

We need to control, filter, and measure our words, for it is easy to launch words for all to hear, but impossible to take them back. It is sad and unfortunate because parents especially women who should educate their children, be role models and show good examples have lost it.

As I write this today, Thursday, September 13th 2018, is a very sad day for me. It is sad because it is the funeral of one of my best friends for over forty years who passed away on August 21st 2018. It was a wakeup call for me once again. It reminded me of how short life is and to be prepared at all times. Never leave what you can do today for tomorrow, because tomorrow may never come. I have experienced deaths of many close to me, like my son, husband, and parents, but I still have my doubts about being dead and gone forever. I have this strong feeling and belief that I will bump into one of them someday. However, as a Christian, physical death means the beginning of eternal life in the presence of God, so I must forget about seeing any of them. I pray that the soul of Carmen Steele rests in perfect peace. Amen.

EARLY CHURCH ACTIVITIES

With regards to church activities, my parents were staunch Catholics, and they would not have it otherwise. My mum belonged to many groups including St Theresa, Legion of Mary, Christian Mothers and Catholic Women Organisation. I am not involved in such activities at this stage of my life because those days were not like now, where females can be Mass Servers. In those days only males were allowed to be Mass Servers and Eucharistic Ministers.

However, the attendance of Benediction and other church services kept us very busy and close to our Catholic faith. It also helped to shape my life, as you will see later in this book. I attended Catholic primary and Catholic Teacher Training. So, it was Catholic school throughout for me. All my siblings attended both primary and secondary Catholic schools. In my early years, I didn't feel like I missed out on anything nor have any regrets I can remember. I met with my friends in school, and we also met up on Sundays. As for Saturdays, when my mum comes to the stall at midday, my shift in her stall kind of comes to an end and she takes over. Then I was free to meet with my friends.

At home, my responsibilities towards my siblings were almost like those of a second mother. I prepared food for everybody. For example, if we were going to make a new soup, my mother would send me home to boil the meat, and if it was okra soup, I would have to chop up the okra and set it aside. I would also have to sort the fish and grind the pepper. If it was *egusi* soup, I would have to grind the *egusi* and set it aside. If it was bitter leaf soup, I would have to wash the bitter leaves, boil and pound the cocoyam and set aside as well. So once all was prepared, my mother would only come home and put them in the pot to cook. That was where I watched and learnt to cook. I did not go to any special school to learn how to cook our food; it was all from helping my mother. And when she was ready to pound; for example, yam for yam *fufu,* I would get my dad's nephew who lived with us to do the manly job that was pounding the yam.

I still believe that in today's climate, it would have been seen as child labour.. Social Services would have been visiting our house daily, that is if they have not bundled my siblings and me into Local Authority care.

The age gap between my immediate younger brother and me is eight years. My mother had a few miscarriages. It was never her plan to have such a gap in-between her children as you can see with the rest of my siblings who were born two years apart.

One might think my mother's parents left her some kind of inheritance since she was a princess. I guess it really does depend. For example, if you looked at the royal family, when Princess Ann got married to her husband, she did not want any of the titles. And moreover, back in Nigeria especially in Igbo land in those days, the girls did not have anything in terms of inheritance per se. Women were not even entitled to inherit property from their fathers. They just happened to be born there. But if she married into a royal family, then it was different. So, obviously, if you marry into an ordinary family, that was it. My mother could not be bothered with royalty or not. All she wanted was to care for her family.

As a devout Christian, she supported my dad at the helm of the affairs for the establishment of our community church- St Jude's Catholic Church, Umudala village as well as St. Anthony's Catholic Church, Nanka. She and my dad dedicated their life to the service of God and ensured that we their children were also deeply rooted in the activities of our religious pillar, no matter where we resided.

My parents shared 56 years of marital bliss, now they have passed on and joined again in death to continue their married life. They both shared a beautiful loving life together, that on one occasion my father could not resist saying that in his next life, 'he will walk the same path way to meet my mother again'.

At 91years and five months, I felt my mother's life should be celebrated as well as mourned, because life gone is life lost forever. We called her "*MAMA ANYI.*" We miss her so much, "but we shall not mourn like those who do not have hope." We would instead rejoice and celebrate the fulfilled and accomplished life which she lived on earth and the achievement that God crowned her with. I held a big Wake for her in London surrounded by my children, grandchildren, family and friends before leaving for Nigeria.

When I arrived in Nigeria, I paid my respect to her in the mortuary and could not believe as I observed her mortal remains lying stiff as the soul has departed to the Creator. I touched her and there was no response, I then realised truly as Shakespeare called it, "a necessary end that will come when it will come." The Apologetics of the Christian Doctrine called it "a moment on which our whole eternity depends". And we call it DEATH- the debt which all mortals must pay, irrespective of age, religion, gender, economic status, societal standing and race.

Growing up from about ten to twenty years of age was filled with many memories and oooh, a lot of them. I don't know if I really have any favourites. I think my fondest period was probably leaving home to attend Teachers' Training College at the age of fifteen. I suppose it was just the element of being independent and getting out of your parent's presence and control. Anyways, no one should be surprised or shocked at my comment because this happens a lot with children these days who even without any genuine reason, just cannot wait to leave home. As a teenager living with her parents, the chance of going to Teachers Training in Akwanga, Plateau State and live with my mates as a boarder was exciting. I was not running away, but it felt like I was finally about to be my own boss.

I think that would be my favourite memory. It was sad leaving home of course, but overall it was kind of a sweet-sour experience leaving home and being my own boss. It was an experience! It was nice because number one, I did not miss my parents even though we were close. However, I missed all of my siblings. This was probably because I was moving on into another phase in my life. It was not like I did not miss my parents per se or that I did not want to be with them but for some reason, I just noted that another phase had come in my life. And again, with the new people I had met, I was trying to establish a relationship with them. So, it was like I had to concentrate on the new era that I had just gone into.

I looked forward to going home for the holidays because when I get home, I would be treated like a princess, and it felt really good. Also, when I was returning to school, my parents bought all sorts of things for me to go with.

Do I have any regrets with this stage of my life? The only regret would probably be not being able to finish my teacher training at Akwanga which was interrupted by the uprising in Northern Nigeria that led to the Biafran civil war. I was in the middle of the third year of a five-year course. It was very sad. My family had to leave for the East to start adjusting, getting to know the environment, making new friends and resettling. People fled, leaving behind friends and collections of years of personal belongings to go back to their place of origin. It was both emotionally and physically daunting. It did disrupt our education a lot. When we got back from Northern Nigeria, it took the whole of three good months to enrol and stabilize. Fortunately, there was Loretta Teachers Training College in our neighbouring town called Adazi, and that was where I continued my course in Teachers Training.

People are always blaming their circumstances for what they are. I don't believe in circumstances. The people who get on in this world are the people who get up and look for the circumstances they want, and if they can't find them, make them.

– George Bernard Shaw

Chapter Three

MY PARENTS

MY DAD

My late father was "*Ichie,*" the highest traditional chieftaincy title in the "*Ozo*" traditional chieftaincy institute. His name thus was "*Ichie* Fidelis Ezeasor." His title name was *Okwuolisa*, which translates as "The Word of The Lord".

My dad was a wonderful man. I was extremely close to him. As far as I was concerned, my father could do no wrong. I have very great respect for him. The quality I loved most about my dad was his exceptional ability to think outside the norm. Inasmuch as my dad was from a community where more emphasis laid on bringing up boys, my dad was someone who believed in gender equality. He had five boys and two girls and trained us all equally to the best of his capability. Remember, I was the eldest of his children. While he was seeing me through school, his friends kept asking him, "Why are your training and sending her to school?" They said, "You could use that money to train the boys. After all, she'll get married and all that money spent would have been wasted." And my dad would turn around and say to them, "You know what? After I've trained her and when she gets married, if her husband doesn't want her to work, she can stay at home, but she can use all her knowledge to make sure she helps her children with their homework. And that way she'd be able to educate her children at home." My father believed that the quality of every human being, man or woman, is fundamentally, essentially and unquestionably equal to the dignity of mankind.

I was extremely close to my dad. I think I share a resemblance to his mum because he called me "*Nne*" (meaning mother – used as a pet name). You know the connection and love fathers have towards their daughters and mothers towards their sons. As my parents aged, I began to travel to Nigeria yearly. Sometimes I visited twice a year, and I made sure one of the trips was during Christmas.

I have a lot of friends in Nigeria, and whenever I visit, I tend to run around from one city to the other visiting my friends. But as my parents aged, I decided that if I go home, I would spend most of my time with them rather than running around visiting friends.

As the years went by, I warned and pleaded with my brothers to keep me posted with our parent's general health. I told them that if for any reason our dad was not feeling well and they know he was very ill, they had to let me know, and not hide it until it was too late.

I am glad my brothers took my instruction to heart. As a result, when my dad was very ill, they called me. They told me that he was not feeling well and he was in the hospital. I asked if I could talk to him, but they said he was quite breathless and when his breathing settles, then I could talk to him. I asked if they were sure he was still alive? They said he was. I asked to speak with his doctor. When my father's doctor came on the phone, he confirmed that my father was still alive. The doctor said that once he regains his breath and strength, they would call me so I could speak with him, and that was precisely what they did.

When he got strong enough to speak, they called me. It was on a Saturday morning, and I spoke with him. I called him "Papa *anyi* (Our Papa) I'm coming." He asked, "*Nne,* are you coming?" And I said, "yes, I'm coming."

After speaking with my dad, I hurried to the travel agents and made plans for a flight ticket. They told me tickets were very expensive during that period. I said, "listen, I've got only one dad, and he's not very well, look for a ticket for me." They found me a ticket, and I paid over one thousand pounds for it at the time as it was urgent, and I needed the ticket that day. Thank God for credit card.

By Monday, two days later I was on the flight to Nigeria. Before leaving, I called my friend at work and asked her to tell my manager that my dad was not well, so I was taking an emergency sick leave to see my dad in Nigeria.

On the same Monday night, I was beside my dad's hospital bed. That was the greatest joy that I ever had in my life. It helped me a lot to cope with him not being around anymore because I was able to be with him during that period. Later that night, my brother said we should go home and come back the next day. "I said home? I came to see my dad. I'm a nurse, and my dad encouraged me to do nursing. Now I've come to give him some much-needed tender loving care - TLC. And you are talking about sleeping in a comfortable bed when my dad is ill and in a hospital bed. I might as well go back to London for my comfortable bed."

Before I left for Nigeria, I had packed some Johnson's baby powder, shaving sticks, baby oil and all the things we used to care for the elderly in the wards in London. I was now ready to go and care for my daddy the same way. When my brothers were going to shave him, I said no, I could shave my daddy.

The next day, I shaved my dad, gave him a blanket bath and all those things that we learned in nursing school. I was so pleased that I had the opportunity to care for him in the hospital with the skills of "care of the elderly" that I acquired during my nursing training. When I finished, I oiled his skin with baby oil and powdered him with Johnson's baby powder. It was such a delight, and I was proud of myself to shower my nursing skills on my dad at that critical period. He was the one who wanted me to go into the nursing profession in the first place. I have no doubt that he was happy, we chattered, he blessed my family and I with words of wisdom and I felt fulfilled and accomplished.

The doctors were fully aware that I had come from London, and they were very helpful. The nurses, however, thought they knew better. I went to the nurses the next day to ask to see my dad's note, and the nurses said, "Oh no, we're not allowed to give the patients or their families the note." I said listen, I came from London, and I want to read my dad's note. They refused. So, I said "Okay, that is fine. When the doctor comes, I'd like to see him."

When the doctor came to see my dad, we exchanged greetings, and he immediately said to me, "Oh Mrs Anolue, it's nice to see you. I heard you're a nursing sister in London." I said yeah. And he said, "Wow, you are the big nurse!" He asked, "Have you seen your daddy's notes?" I said "no, your nurses wouldn't let me. They said that it's not allowed." The doctor turned around and said to the nurses, "What do you mean she can't read the notes? Do you know that this woman is one of the real nurses we talk about?" And he went on to tell them off.

After all the fuss, I was allowed to read my dad's note which was quite straight forward. On looking through his medical history, I must say it was not bad for an 86-year-old man. My father, like my mum, had regular medical check-ups and I am proud to say they were never in-patients at the hospital until the tail end of their lives.

I gave him blanket baths almost every day. I stayed in Nigeria for ten days, and I spent all that time at the hospital. The nurses were shocked to see that this woman from England was sleeping on the floor with just a mat and no mattress. My parents, especially my mother taught me humility and letting the hair down and never being pompous.

I told them that he was my dad. Besides, if my mum had been sleeping there all this while, why couldn't I? I was even happy to relieve my mum so she could go back home where it was more comfortable to rest.

After spending ten wonderful, happy days with my dad and giving him all the well needed and deserved TLC, I returned to London to continue with my life here.

Exactly ten days after I returned to London, I vividly remember that something happened that I believe was very significant to show how close I was with my dad. It happened on a Friday night. The reason why the memory was so vivid was that I had one of my goddaughters' wedding ceremony the next day being a Saturday. On this Friday night at about 10.30pm, I became quite restless. This was in September 2003. I called my youngest daughter and told her that I was very restless and I did not know what it was. I could not pinpoint what was making me restless. She asked, "But mummy, are you worried?" I said, "no, I'm not worried, but something is making me restless."

At about 11 pm I said to her, let me go and sit in the bath with a lot of bubbles to make me relax. I asked her to come with me to help wash my back and talk to me. As I sat in the bath, I was calm, but something kept bothering me, and I could not tell what it was. I stayed in the tub for almost two hours.

When I got out of the bath and dried myself, I was still wide awake. I think by now it was around 2 am, when my brother in Canada called me and said, "Woman, are you still awake?" I said, "yes, I don't know, but I'm so restless, and I don't know what it is." He said, "You are not an early sleeper anyway". I said yes, but in normal circumstances, I don't get restless like this. He said, "Anyway, since it's already past 2, am let's not talk too much, you try and get some sleep." I said okay. So, I went to bed and tried to go to sleep, but by 5 am I was wide awake. That meant that I probably had less than three hours of sleep. So I got up and started doing things.

At about 6 am on Saturday, my immediate younger brother from Nigeria called. I asked him, "how come you're calling so early, is there any problem?" He said, "No, I woke up early and I thought just to call you because I was meant to call you last week and I fell asleep." At the time, I did not know that he was looking for a flimsy excuse for calling. He then asked why I was up that early. I said, well I could not sleep last night and we had a wedding to attend today. I was supposed to drive and I feel very tired and I did not know how I was going to drive. Everybody was coming in my car, so I had to try. He said to me, "Why don't you call the people you are going with and see if someone else can drive since you are tired." I said there was nobody else to drive and that was the reason I offered to so there was no need to bother calling them. But after that, I thought to myself, I'm not sure if I can drive, why don't I tell them?"

So, I decided I would call the family I was going with to the wedding. When I called, I told them that I would not be able to drive to the wedding because I was very tired. Before I could finish speaking the lady said, "Oh Kate, it's amazing, I was actually going to call to say my son would be driving so you don't have to bother about driving us." So, I said, okay, that's fantastic, thank you very much. I continued by saying, in that case, I'm going to bring my head tie and come to you to tie my *gele.* I went to their house and I was relieved that I did not have to drive.

When we finished tying my *gele*, I went home to get dressed. After getting dressed, they came to pick me up, and we drove to my goddaughter's wedding. When we got there, even with one of my favourite artist's music playing (Michael Jackson), I still could not dance. I was still feeling very down. They asked me, "Oh Kate what's the matter? You're not your usual merry self." I said nothing, but I could feel something was not right. I said to them, you know what? I'm going home. And they said," What? After all, this is your goddaughter's wedding." I said, if you're not ready to leave, I'll go get a bus or taxi. Then they said, "Okay if that's the case we can't let you go alone since we all came together. I'll tell my friend, the bride's mother that we're going home." So, they went and spoke to the bride's mum, and we were off.

When we reached the North Circular road, at the junction of Fore Street, Edmonton, I told them that I would love to be let out here, so that they could go straight home. They said, "Oh no, we'll come with you since we left the party early." I said, "aah, that's nice! It was the first time we would all be together to enjoy tea. In those days, I used to drink tea like fish in water. Not now anymore, I gave up tea and coffee fourteen years ago.

When we got back to my house, I found my eldest daughter Didi at home. I asked her, Ndidi, what are you doing at home She said, "Oh mummy, auntie phoned me to say one of her daughters studying law wanted some information and I thought rather than phoning and talking over the phone, I'll come home." I said that's good, let's make some tea and enjoy.

As the tea was getting ready, my cousin called and said, "Oh aunty, I just wanted to know if you have Amaechi's number?" I thought to myself, that's odd, but I said no since I did not have it then. Then he said to me, "It's okay. I'm coming around anyway." I asked if everything was alright. He said, "Yes aunty, I'm just around the corner going to my friend's place."

With all these building up, I began to suspect something was not right. And that was when Engineer Cyril Ibekwe, the husband of my friend whose son drove us to the wedding asked me to sit down. As soon as the words came out, I screamed yes, that's it my dad was gone; my dad was gone! I knew it! I knew it! He was calling me and hovering around me from 10.30pm the previous night throughout as he was passing on I was restless. Now I know why. I did not have to ask any more questions. I already knew what was wrong with me.

I am a sound sleeper. I sleep quite easily, and nothing wakes me up. Even when I wake, I quickly fall back asleep. But that was the night I could not sleep. Now I know I could not sleep because as my dad's spirit was leaving his body, it was hovering around me until he passed on.

Now, all of them were aware that my dad had passed away and all they were trying to do was get together to tell me knowing full well how close I was to my dad. And also, my restless night was because of my dad; my dad was passing on and hovering around me. I was feeling the death of my father. Hence, the restlessness which began around 10.30pm and my dad died at exactly 11 pm that night.

Cyril Ibekwe from Nanka as myself, his wife Eucharia and their son were all in my house. My brother from Canada kept calling; I suppose to check if I had been told about our father's death. He knew that I had not been told because I spoke with him normally the night before. My brother calling from Nigeria, and my eldest daughter Didi coming home just to give information to my friend's daughter was too much of a coincidence. It all made sense once they broke the news of my dad passing on. They wanted to be around to comfort me, and I am grateful to them and appreciate them immensely.

My dad passed on aged 86 in September 2003 at 11 pm, exactly ten days after I returned to London. I miss him but also, I thank God that I was able to see him in the hospital and gave him tender loving care. I will always miss him because he had been extremely involved in my life.

I thank my dad very much for my education. My dad was someone who believed in gender equality, and he believed that women should be given the opportunity to be educated, and that was why I could never give up on anything I embarked on.

I owe this to my father because if he were like the other men around then, I probably would not be here today. I would probably be making up the statistics of girls not educated. My father is somebody who I can never forget. He was my role model. I owe all my achievements to my father, and I dedicate all awards and honours to him and my late husband who also kept his promise to my dad by allowing me to continue with my education while fulfilling my wifely duties.

My life's motto is: "Nursing is my vocation but empowering women is my mission". I think it all came through my dad. I aim to empower women through those words, and I believe that as a woman, I should also be encouraging other women to make sure that they don't get left behind. Most men believe that training women is a waste of time because they see them as house commodity and kitchen equipment etc. Unfortunately, some women believe this too; so they don't make any efforts to enlighten themselves, even when the opportunities present themselves.

MY MUM

My mum was a disciplinarian. She was hard. I do not think I inherited any of that gene from my mother. And I am glad that I did not. I believe I am more like my dad. I am a disciplinarian but not a hard one like my mum.

In comparing my mum and dad I know, one person had to be soft while the other had to be hard. And it was the same thing in my marriage. I was the hard one, and my husband was soft. That was how I saw it anyway. And because I was very close to my dad, I got away with a lot of mischief. If my mum told me off, I would do nothing. I just waited until my dad was almost home for the day. When my dad is coming back in the evening, you could tell because he enjoyed whistling. He whistled instead of singing. So as soon as my dad steps in whistling, gosh! I would start crying. It could have been that my mum told me off hours and hours ago. I probably would have finished grumbling, but I needed somebody to get my mother sorted out. It is terrible the things children do even though they do not realise it.

For my mum to have told me off, obviously I would have done something wrong or failed to do something she had asked me to do. It could have been that she went out and told me to grind *egusi* (melon seeds) then I got too busy playing and forgot to get it done. And yes, I had a lot of time to play.

After she comes back, she would tell me off. After telling me off, I would start crying. After crying, then I would go to do it. As soon as my dad's arrival approaches, I would start crying again. Then my dad would come to console me and call me by my pet name, "*Nne, Nne*" and ask me what was wrong. I would say it's Mama *anyi* (our mama) as I called my mum. Then I would stop crying and wait to see the result. The result was usually that my dad would tell my mother off. Then I would be happy. They could even argue because of me, and I would feel pleased with myself.

But now I realise that what I was causing then could be seen by some as domestic violence in this twenty-first century, and it is sad because I caused these rows because they made me feel better. Then they would quarrel and quarrel and I would sit in one corner, all the while making a mockery of my mum happily. What a brat I was. As a mother, I brought this up with my mother as a discussion. I was glad to see that she did not comment much on those incidents. She merely saw them as part of growing up; innocent acts of a spoilt brat. I just laughed. I could not even apologise as she did not think there was any reason to apologise. Maybe it was because we read too many meanings into our actions these days, I wondered. Anyways, the most important thing was that my parents loved each other and shared 56 wonderful years of marriage.

I did some other things to cause my parents to argue. When I was about 16 -18 years old, I usually go home with my childhood friend, Lina from Loretto Adazi Teachers Training College for a weekend break. Because I loved yam and we had a yam barn, I would go to take the yams that I liked from the barn. If my dad was not there, my mum would ask me to drop the yams I picked and ask me to take smaller yams. I would say no, I don't want those and my mum would say "if you don't want those, then stay there because you won't get any." I would argue by telling her that if she did not give me the ones that I wanted, then I would not go back to school. She would say "you'll be late." And I would respond that I did not care. Then, I would wait for my dad to come back.

So you see how stubborn I was and still am? I would wait until my dad came home and he would ask, "Eh, *Nne*, haven't you gone back?" I would answer "no, our mother refused to give me yam." He would ask, "But what do you mean?" I would respond that it was because she would not let me take the yams that I wanted. He would immediately say, "*Nne*, come with me." Then I would hurry behind him to the barn. Once there, he would ask, "Which ones do you want?" and I would point to the ones I wanted, and he would just tell me to take them. So, with my dad, I could get away with murder.

Sometimes, I would go home on a Saturday to take my younger sister who was about four or five then – Louie *Nne* (as I always call her), so she could stay with us in school till Sunday. We had to hide her because the Reverend Sisters went around the dormitories at night. All my friends loved her. She could be sleeping on one of our beds, and you would not be able to tell which. As the Head Girl, the girls always supported me because they all knew how I loved my only sister dearly. They would even plait her hair and shower her with presents every time I brought her to spend some time with me.

You are a child of God. Your playing small does not serve the world. There is nothing enlightened about shrinking so that other people won't feel insecure about you. We were born to manifest the glory of God that is within us.

-Marianne Williamson

Chapter Four

COMING TO ENGLAND

Truth be told, I had no motivation to come to England. I happened to get married, and it was an arranged marriage. The way it worked out was that since we lived in the Northern part of Nigeria, I always went to the East during the holidays. I had a cousin who lived in Enugu, Eastern Nigeria and worked with the Ministry of Information. We met with his family while on holidays from Jos where we lived as of then. In 1964, during my first year in Teachers Training School, we went on a Christmas holiday to Enugu. From there, we all went home to the village for the Christmas holiday.

So once in the village, I happened to be seen by one of my dad's friend from Anolue's family. Later, I understood that he went to ask my father's brother about who I was. He was told that I was Fidelis' daughter. So, he said he had a nephew who lived in England who was looking for a wife, and said he needed to speak with my parents. By the way, no one thought about speaking to me about any of this, I must add. I must have been about fourteen or fifteen years old as of then.

So, he went to speak with my dad's brother. My uncle told him that it was okay and everything would be fine. My uncle had agreed without even talking to my parents first. Yes, my dad's brother agreed because I was staying with his son who worked at the Ministry of Information and I did not even know. After all these things were discussed and done; the war broke out and my family had to move back home to the East.

Next thing I knew, they had come to my parents to do what they call laying down of wine, "*ha bialu donye mmanya*". This meant that they had come to make marriage *Introduction*. It's almost like I was now betrothed to them. So, in a way, I was now engaged. When this happens, you are kind of stuck there. My husband's cousins and parents did all these while he was in the UK.

Then he sent his pictures and messages. During these times, there were no public facilities for international phones, just letters, and telegrams. We wrote letters. There were lots of letters coming and going. This was when the war had just started.

During the war, there were a lot of people around. I had my childhood friend, and I enjoyed going to their town called Nimo. I always joined their student meetings, and there was this young chap who would always ask about me. My friend told him, "You better don't bother. She's already engaged."

It cost me a lot you know, especially with the people I met afterwards. But for some reason, the word "*Obodo Oyibo*" (The Whiteman's Country) overshadowed everything. I did not feel like I was trapped anymore. I knew that when the time comes, I'll go to the Whiteman's Country. So that was how I got myself into this Whiteman's country business. It was like I was engaged forever because of the civil war. It however gave me the opportunity to continue my teacher's training anyway. So, by the time I came to England I was already twenty years old and it was okay. The only thing was that I did not know him as well as I would have wanted.

How do you get on with someone you have never seen, spoken to or even met? There was nothing like Facebook or the telephone. We were like pen pals who wrote a lot of letters and exchanged photographs. I did not like it that way, but it was typical for that period.

If I could go back or reverse things, I would have loved to make the choice myself. However, I'm very lucky that I was married to a very nice person. Yes, I was lucky because he was a very kind and loving man. This was the aspect I would say I was lucky. Other than that, I did not think it was a good idea. If you were going to marry somebody and settle with them for life, you need the opportunity to get to know that person. You need to learn their character, their ways, exchange conversations and see how that person judges things and so forth. I was thrown in with somebody I did not know and never met in my life. It was not a very good thing to do. It was an arranged marriage, but thank God young people now have the opportunity to make their choices these days. We know there are still some countries in the continents of Asia and Africa where this is still practiced.

MY HUSBAND

I had one year to complete my teacher training before leaving for England. The school was closed due to the war, and we were not sure when it would be reopened. So while waiting, we began applying for my visa to join my husband in England. The plan was that if the school re-opened before my visa was ready, I would complete my final year before leaving. If the visa was granted before the school re-opened, then I would leave for England. I was just about to leave Nigeria when the school resumed; roughly about February or March 1971. It was apparent that the travelling plans had gained the upper hand.

I arrived in England in May 1971. My husband came for me at the airport. I did not have to think about what he looked like because we had been exchanging photographs for a long time. So, it was easy to recognise him.

He was a very handsome man, about ten years older than me. He worked at a top men's suit maker called Norton & Sons in Savile Row, making hand-made men's suits. These days one would call him a fashion designer. At the time, you would pay over a thousand pounds for a hand-made suit. It was also very exciting for me when I met Andrew Ramroop OBE, owner and founder of Maurice Sedwell in Savile Row. He reminded me of when my late husband was working for Norton & Sons and later went on to become self-employed, but remained with Norton & Sons. It is only now that I appreciate the location and where he worked, "The West End."

With my education in mind, my dad gave one condition to my husband's family when they came for the marriage *Introduction.* He explicitly told them that I was still a student and that he, my dad was prepared to sponsor me up to whatever level I wanted. However, if they were keen to marry me, since the man was still over there and I was very young, it was fine as long as I would be allowed to continue with my education. They agreed, and that was why my dad did not object to the marriage. So, I was able to carry on with my education. May I remind you all that I only learnt about the details of the arrangement later in life. It was never discussed with me, and neither did anyone ask for my opinion. My rights to consent were taken away from me.

Now in England, before I could even remind my husband about schooling, he said "Oh, I know your dad wanted you to get back into school, and there's no problem at all. And also, your dad wanted you to be a nurse, and that's fine too." I said, okay, that's good. Then I started looking for a school of nursing. Back then, we lived in South West London. My husband had a family friend who lived in North London then and still does even until now. They were his very good friends. I call them my pen pals because we used to exchange letters and I got to know them very well even without seeing them.

They gave me the address of North Middlesex Hospital so I could apply. I applied and because I had a very good background education and intelligence, allow me to copy President Donald Trump's words; I would say "I'm very smart,' - when they gave me their test papers, they were quite easy for me, so I finished quickly with top marks.

I have always been capable of multitasking effectively, and I do not know when I am going to stop. I arrived in May, and by May of the following year, I was in a school of nursing, and I had one child already. Yes, I had my first daughter in 1972.

The school of nurse training has changed from what it used to be. Back, then it was just an ordinary school of Nursing where you completed your three-year training and be certified as a State Registered Nurse. All the theory was in the hospital lecture room and practical in the ward. Since nursing has been made into a degree, there are now more lectures at the University and less practical, very much out of touch with the patients while training.

In the first year of schooling, you had to live in the nurses' home. It was not convenient for me as I was a married woman. Even when my husband came to visit, he was not allowed into the room. We met downstairs at the reception, and we would spend one, two or three hours there. Visitors were not allowed to come into our rooms. This was not good at all for the married student nurses then, but then it did not matter much to me as I was on a mission and I knew why I was there and where I was heading. So, I just looked forward to my days off duty.

By the time I completed my first year, we were able to buy our own house in 1972. We moved from Balham, South London to Edmonton in North London as homeowners, with a mortgage. It was a great achievement for my husband and especially me as I had barely spent two years in London. As soon as we bought our first house, our daughter who was living with foster parents for a brief period joined us. I still had to live in the nurses' home in my second year but my third and final years were great as I travelled from my home.

Once again, I had a childminder who looked after my daughter on days when I had to work. It was a tough decision, but if you needed your qualification in those days while building your family, that was the norm. On my days off, which were two, sometimes three days, I would go to visit my daughter and bring her home so that we could have a lovely family time together. It was not a problem, the way we saw it back then. It was the practice among most Nigerians as they studied for their future. Today, I congratulate and almost envy the young couples as they are lucky to have grandparents and in some cases, I have seen, great grandparents helping out with childcare. I am also very happy that young dads of today are very keen to be involved with antenatal, parenting education and care of their children. As a midwife, I encouraged this practice, and I see the benefits everywhere. I still can visualise my son-in-law putting nappy on and dressing his little princess within the first few hours of her birth in labour ward. This is a far cry from my father and forefathers; I know for a fact that back in Nigeria, it remains a woman's job predominantly.

My husband was also very involved with my antenatal care. As first-time parents, we both went to antenatal and parenting classes. We were very fortunate as some of our family friends were Midwives and Health Visitors, so we had the best of advice and support.

While I was in my final year in the School of Nursing, I always took my daughter to the childminder every morning. Anyways, we worked it out between the both of us. At Norton & Sons in Savile Row, my husband was self-employed, and he had flexibility with his working hours. He was able to go in late or early and leave early or late as he pleased. It was a lot of juggling, but we were both very determined. I was able to concentrate on my studies, and I had no problem with that. Fortunately, nurses' off duty shifts were made weeks ahead, making it extremely easy for us to plan for when my husband could go in to work early or late. I passed all my exams with flying colour. Within five years of arriving in the United Kingdom, I had gained two certificates; State Registered Nurse and State Certified Midwife, two children, and of course our own mortgaged home.

Settling in England had its ups and downs. I did not like the cold weather. The cold weather was a shock to my system, especially during winter when it got very cold. You know how sometimes when you wash your clothes and you put them out to dry and it is nice and crispy, but somehow, it is still wet! I did not like the snow either. I fell over quite a few times. But fortunately, there were no injuries; I suppose it was because I was young and strong. If I ever fall now, my bones would be broken beyond repair, so I am now mindful of my steps and movements. By the way, just so you know, when it comes to dancing, nothing can stop me. I love dancing. You could say dancing is my vice.

My husband had a lot of friends, and they were very good to me. They also helped to integrate me into the system. Besides, I had also exchanged letters with some of them while I was in Nigeria, so in some ways, it was like seeing your senior pen pals face to face.

So, settling down was not too bad. But because we had just gone through a civil war, it was a good move for me. Also, because he allowed me to do the things that I wanted to do or that my parents wanted me to do, there were no regrets.

My husband was one of the top men's suit designers in Nigeria. Like most Nigerians those days, he came over to England to study and obtain a Diploma Certificate in tailoring, and he ended up staying because of the civil war. Even after the civil war ended, the country was still unstable. Our young family also started to expand, and so it was difficult to go back at that time.

MY CHILDREN

My first child was a girl, the second a boy, the third who is deceased was also a boy. I had to mention him because he was a full-term birth weighing 8lbs 6ozs. He lived for less than twenty-four hours before passing away in the hospital. This is something we call a cot death in the medical profession. Then came the fourth a boy and finally my youngest, a girl. Cot death is the worst thing I could wish for anybody, not even my worst enemy if I had any. To go through a full-term pregnancy, shopping for baby clothes and preparing older children for baby's arrival and then having to cope with the loss and emotions. There were also the mounting unanswered questions from within you. These are just a few of the challenges one had to face.

I had my children with four-year gaps between them. The one that would have been a three-year gap was Okeychukwu, born in 1989. Unfortunately, I had the pleasure of enjoying his company in this world for a very short period. It was in the following year I had Chukwuma.

BECOMING A YOUNG WIDOW

All of my children were relatively young when their dad passed away. The youngest was eighteen months old, and others were five, nine and thirteen years old respectively. As a multitasking person that I am; I was now acting as a mother, father, career person and a homemaker.

My husband had an accident and died at the young age of 46. The first thought that ran through my mind after he passed was wow, what am I going to do with all these children alone? The second thought was, I'm just going to take them back to Nigeria with me. The third thought was, I'll bring my mum to stay with me. But then again, how would that work since my dad was still alive? The fourth thought was, I think I'll leave everything to the Lord because from where I come from, we have a saying that the Lord does not give you a cross you cannot carry.

So, I believed that this was my cross and I had to carry it; I had to find a way to deal with it. And that was how I started thinking positively, and I started believing that I could do it. I had a few older mothers who said the same thing to me. They said, "Kate, it's not more than you. God looked at you and knew that you could carry that cross, and that's why he gave it to you. Carry it and carry it with pride; you shall be alright." Those words echoed in my mind, and they brought me comfort and encouragement in my time of despair.

So, I had been thrown into the deep end. I had to learn to swim to survive or not swim and sink. I had to carry that cross with pride as my friends had said. So, I said to myself, I had to learn to carry this cross properly before it became too heavy that I would not be able to manage. From that moment on, I never looked back.

I learned that courage was not the absence of fear, but the triumph over it. The brave man is not he who does not feel afraid, but he who conquers that fear.

– Nelson Mandela

Chapter Five

LONE PARENTHOOD HERE I COME

I do not think that anybody prays to raise their children alone. Sometimes though, things happen that forces one to end up being a lone parent. I had just become one of those people.

Most people would run to the Council to get help either financially or otherwise, but I did not. I didn't get any financial support from the Council or anything. I did not even go to them. I'm someone who thinks that I have to try my best before asking for help. That was just my belief. So, I did not get any financial support from them per se. One positive thing they did for me, however which was much better than finances was making sure that my youngest child had a place in the nursery, free of charge. The rest of the children had free school meals, so I did not have to worry about that. I think all those things in kind were also indirectly financial help. They were all of massive help to me above all else. The rest of the expenses, I bore out of my pocket. I relied majorly on my profession.

At work, I did what we called "On Call". So, I went to see my head of community midwifery to negotiate for more flexible working hours. Before I could open my mouth to speak, she said: "Kate, look at the shifts and see what you'd like and we'll discuss about it." She made my life easy. That is why I always say; "wherever you are, especially in your place of work, make sure that your slate is clean." Leave your slate clean so that you can leave the door open for others and yourself because you never know when you will need to pass through that door again. I was happy because I had a good rapport with them. So, it was easy for me to get resettled at work when I resumed.

So now, my head of community midwifery had sorted out my duty days. I had a nursery for the youngest child, and I took the rest of the children to school. The childminder picked them up from school, and everything appeared to be running smooth. On my "On Call" days, some of my friends who had teenage children allowed their children to come and stay in my house in case I was called out. That was how I coped. I had good friends around, and as the saying goes, "A friend in need is a friend indeed."

Whatever I write in this paragraph would not do justice to my experience of being a young widow and lone parent as it would take another book to recount my whole experience; the agony, emotional, psychological stress of it all. I do hope that I would be able to put these in writing sometime, as a follow-up.

As I have mentioned earlier, the nursing I did was to please my dad because that was what he wanted me to do. He even went to the extent of warning my husband to make sure that I became a nurse. He said, "If she can't do nursing, please leave her. When I am done training her, you can come back. If she's still there, then you can talk about marrying her." I am eternally grateful to my dad for getting me started on a career path that I have used to transform lives and that also has been quite helpful in my own life too.

POLITICAL CAREER BREWING

My midwifery practice was in the community. While working as a community midwife, I met a lot of pregnant women and their families. We had a lot of discussions, and they were very open to me. Some told me of their problems with housing, health, environment, and social services. I'd tell them that I would go to the council and find out who they could meet and then go back to pass the information to them.

Gradually, one day, I asked myself, these people from the council you keep asking things from, who are these people? Have they got two heads? Then I thought to myself that I was going to find out who these people were.

LAW DEGREE CALLING ME

With my youngest just eight years old, many people could not believe that I was a widow with four children, a full-time professional and still wanted to study for a Law degree.

The way I started on my law degree was particularly funny. I took the entrance exam which was specifically for mature students and passed it. They called me for the interview. They had gone through my CV, so they said to me, "You are a practising midwife, what do you want a Law degree for?" I responded; it's my passion. They said, "It's very hard. You are a widow, who looks after your children?" I answered, sometimes my friends. They said, "Even with that, go and think about it." And I said okay and went home.

After two weeks, the University called me back to ask, "Have you thought about it?" I said, yes, I had thought about it. They asked, "What do you want to do?" I said I wanted to study for a Law degree. They insisted by asking, "Are you sure? Can you cope?" I said, yes, of course. Then they said, "Okay." They knew they could not stop me from what I wanted to do. I suppose all of this was because of their pass rate and drop out statistics. If I was admitted and dropped out, I might have deprived somebody else of that place. Anyway, they offered me a place, and I started my Law degree where I studied with young people.

Initially, they tried hard to stop me from doing it because they said it would be very tedious. But I stood my ground and insisted that I wanted to do it and that I could do it. They had no choice but to let me carry on. Now, I was studying for my Law degree and working as a full-time community midwife. This was some miracle that nobody could fathom. It was very hard. At this very moment, I think about it, and I still ask myself how I did it? I do not know. It was a miracle. On this note, I would like to repeat for you to trust and believe in yourself always; be determined even when you are faced with difficult questions and people doubt your capability.

My lectures were on Mondays and Wednesdays at 6 pm. At work, nobody knew exactly what I was doing except for one person. That one person was my friend Blossom Davidson. We had agreed that if at any time I was caught up with delivering a baby or something she would come to take over from me. That was the agreement between us, and no one else knew what we had going on. That was how I carried on with the obsession of studying Law.

So, on Mondays and Wednesdays, immediately I finished from the labour ward, I went straight to my car. The boot of my car was my wardrobe and my library. Everything was there. I did not take them out, except for the ones that I needed for studying that day. I thank God that I could drive. I call my car my husband because it was a very loyal 'husband'. I could plan to do one hundred things, and with the car, I would achieve them all. I believed in my car, and it gave me a lot of service. It helped me to accomplish the things that I wanted to achieve.

I had Fridays off from midwifery. On those Fridays, I went to the University, and I did an additional module. This helped reduce my study years in the university. So, instead of studying for five years, I did four years part-time because I was studying three times a week instead of two. I also had reduced modules due to my Nursing & Midwifery qualification.

By now, the children had grown, and they understood enough about homework and exams. So, we were all busy with our things. They knew that on Mondays, mummy was not at home. I usually arranged their food and everything they might need. All they had to do was warm it in the microwave when they returned. When I returned, we would study together. I found time to do their homework with them. Once they finished, I would take my books to my room, and that was where I did my study. And this was the practice in our house for four good years.

When I finished my Law degree, I took my certificate to my head of midwifery and told her that I would like her to update my CV. She looked at it and said, "What's this?" I said, yeah, that's me. She was so shocked. She asked, "How did you do it?" One thing I knew that she did was to go through my record to see whether I had been taking time off or sick days. But, touch wood, one thing that I am blessed with is extremely good health. The only drugs that I was using were multivitamins intermittently and paracetamol or ibuprofen for lower back pain; something almost all nurses suffer "Occupational hazard". I was just fortunate.

So, once I had shown her my certificate, she had to update my profile. She still marvels on how I did it. I wish I could tell her, but I did not know either.

I got my Law degree certificate in 1997. Then I asked myself, now that you've achieved your aim, what do you want to do? Do you want to stop the midwifery and go on with Law?" At that point, I did not know what I wanted.

So, I went to the University of Westminster where I applied to study for one year at the School of Law. The school fee was so much, and I thought to myself that I could not afford this. As of then, it was about £7000. There were also a few questions they asked that I could not answer satisfactorily. The main challenges were the fees and my job. They asked about my living condition, and I said I owned a property. They asked if I had a mortgage and I said yes. They told me that it would be difficult for me to pay the fees, my mortgage and then sort out my other financial obligations. I knew that they were right and I agreed with them. So, that was how I decided I was not going further with the Law career and I would carry on with midwifery.

The only nice thing that I did was to use my legal knowledge to become the Midwives Union Representative. My knowledge has helped me when people get queries about the notes. I would also go to scrutinise and tell them what they had done wrong and what they should have done better and so forth.

POLICTICAL CAREER BEGINNING

When my father learnt about my Law degree, he did not mind because as far as he was concerned, I had achieved what he wanted me to which was becoming a nurse. My siblings, however, were shocked. My brother Dozie, more than others was shocked because he was also a barrister in Nigeria. I had always loved Law, but I could not do it myself because my dad wanted me to do something else; so, I initially felt the other way of achieving this goal was to push my brother Dozie towards it. I also told my eldest daughter that she had to do Law. So, they both heeded and studied Law.

At the moment, my daughter is not practising; she works as a corporate lawyer. Dozie, on the other hand, is a practising barrister. Before Dozie went to Law school, my father did not want to hear of it at all. He said, "It's where people go to learn how to lie. Lawyers know how to lie because something they know is black and they are very sure is black; they can still convince you that it's red." My dad never had anything good to say about lawyers even though he never had any personal encounter with Lawyers.

Studying Law for me was fulfilling. I finally got to do what I always wanted to do. I had satisfied everybody; my father and myself. I must say, however, that midwifery has gone into my marrow and there was no way I could give midwifery up. Giving it up would be like cutting my hands.

Now that I had completed my Law degree, I decided to get into politics. My primary motivation for getting into politics was to solve the problems of my colleagues and clients - the women I serve in the community. Like I mentioned earlier, when people asked me questions at work, I always asked myself if the people I got information from had two heads. I decided that I could do it as well. After all, they knew the officers to ask, and they ask the questions, but they still came to me. I could do the same too. That was one motivation.

The second motivation was that during my inquiries, it seemed like every person in politics was a lawyer. That was why I decided that I wanted to be a lawyer as well. It would serve as my stepping stone into politics. Besides, I could not use the Law degree for anything else that I could think of other than using it in our legal department at North Middlesex hospital to advise on note queries. It was also useful in becoming the Midwives Steward or Union Representative.

COMMUNITY WORK

Since it seemed like all the politicians I knew were lawyers, I could now be one of them with my Law degree. I could join them in arguing about things in politics because I liked to argue too. I loved working in the community also, because before all these I had been deep in the community, working with the Women's Aid at Enfield. For a long time too, I had been working with victims of domestic violence mostly because of the cases I came across in the maternity unit and in the community. I was usually at the forefront and they told me things that they were going through such as emotional, physical, financial abuse and others. So, because of my close and personal relationship with them, they were able to speak out and confide in me.

I had also been very active in my Borough long before I joined in the politics. I used to volunteer at the Youth centre and the Refuge centre. So, I was very busy with these community works, and it was these works that earned me "**Honorary Freeman of the Borough of Enfield.**" award or recognition.

I came to England in 1971 and in 1972, I moved to Enfield, and I still live there. So, I had lived in Enfield for all the time I had spent working here in the UK. I lived in Edmonton for twenty years before moving to Bush Hill Park in 2003, which was also the year that my dad died.

Did getting a Law degree change my life significantly? Well, I did a lot of things at the same time, and I did not know how I did them. I did them because they were things I wanted to do to help change my life.

I finished my Law degree in 1997. And even before then, in 1989 I ran a Nursing Agency from my house. I employed two staff members working part-time. We supplied hospitals with trained and untrained nurses. The nurses and midwives registered with the agency and we provided the hospitals with nurses and midwives when requested. All of these things helped shaped me into who I am today.

As for my children, I do not think any of these affected them. I multitasked efficiently and I sincerely still do not know how I did it. My children did see me and I took them out on my days off. We went to theme parks and the likes. My time off was not just for me alone; it was for the children and me and that was how we did it. So instead of saying, Oh, I'm off today. I'll go and lie down to sleep. Instead, I ask, where shall we go? We might go on outings, and I would take my books with me because we might go with other friends of theirs. When we get there and they start running around, I pick my books and I might read one or two lines. These days, one glues their eyes to the phone, either Tweeting, Facebook, Instagram etc. How things have changed.

Sometimes their friends' parents would come with us and other times they did not. It depends on the plan or arrangement we had in place. I did not make it a habit to take my books, however, except when I had exams coming up.

Our deepest fear is not that we are inadequate.
Our deepest fear is that we are powerful beyond measure.
It is our Light, not our Darkness, that most frightens us.

-Marianne Williamson

Chapter Six

POLITICAL GOALS FOR MY COMMUNITY

When I entered politics, I had one goal, and I still have that goal. My goal was to empower and inspire other women, especially single mothers. You know a lot has been said about single mothers; number one, their children were hopeless; two, they were lazy, and three, the mothers themselves have come to believe that they were lazy and they could not make it.

I wanted to empower them. I wanted to show them that no matter what it was, they could achieve whatever they set their minds to. It all comes down to how they saw themselves. If they saw themselves as lazy, stupid and could not be bothered, that was exactly what they would get. But if they believe in themselves and know what they want to achieve, even if they don't accomplish all, they will achieve enough to be proud of. It might also open doors to something else for them. I like to think that I have inspired them in my time. I made a point of telling my story, no matter how brief, not because I wanted to show off, but to encourage other women to believe in themselves and retain the will power to achieve.

When I was elected into Enfield Council, there were no Nigerian Councillors at the time. However, I made sure that I paved a path for others and now any Nigerian councillor that you might hear about in Enfield, I opened the door for them. I was the one who mentored them.

I was the one who helped them in whatever way; filling forms, advice, things to do, getting in and being a school governor, educating and showing them how campaigning with others would help them too.

I encouraged and advised them to become active members and not just dormant members so that when the elections come, they can come forward to be elected into office as Secretary, Vice Chair, Ethnic Minority Officer or the Women Officer which I was for many years. All these and many more were things I advised them on. I was pleased with myself because for me, I had achieved my goal. There is more work to be done though. There are still not enough ethnic minority people in the Local Government.

I think my other inspiration was that it opened doors for others and me; it also helped me to realise that I could do whatever I set my mind to. In addition, it helped me to form the opinion that when you are 99% positive about yourself and 1% negative, don't be surprised that that 1% would nullify the 99% positivity. You might think that 99% is plenty; you've only just said oh I can't do it, but the moment you've said that, the spirit of that 1% have gone to the 99% and said, oh she said she can't do it. Then you start to struggle and you start wondering why you can't get things together. You need to maintain positivity about yourself, even when things appear impossible. You can also never overemphasise the need for proper time management. I have learnt a lot, and it has helped me abundantly.

I became a Councillor in 2002, and I remained one for ten years. I became Deputy Mayor in my eleventh year on the Council before eventually becoming Mayor in my twelfth year.

Becoming a Mayor was never one of my goals but the opportunity came, and I took it. I am glad that I did because it helped me a lot to build up my self-determination and assertiveness. Although I was always an assertive person, it added more to it.

As a Mayor, you do a lot of things. To start with, I am happy and proud to say that I was the first Nigerian Mayor from the Borough of Enfield. My proudest moment would be my inauguration day. I do not remember seeing other Nigerian Councillors wearing their traditional outfit on the day of their inauguration. On the day of my inauguration, I brought true Africa! I brought true Nigeria! I even wore my *gele* (traditional headscarf). When I walked into that hall that day, it was magnificent. I walked with pride and elegance, showing the beauty of Nigeria, showing the beauty of an African woman. I felt like I was the pride of an African woman showing off her most beautiful complete attire. You know, I noticed that we Africans were not portraying our costumes enough, although it is getting better these days. I was glad that I did on that day.

When I came out, it was like, wow! I brought the WOW factor. And up till now, a lot of people still call me Madam Mayor or Mayor Kate. I am no longer a mayor, but I did put the spice into being a mayor. There were mayors before me, but for some of them, we did not even know when they had their inauguration. We know the year, but the events were usually so quiet. In my time, I made sure it was out there. I reached every single community that I could think.

MAYORAL DUTIES

I went to almost all the Nigerian churches in London. I never turned down any invitations. I went to the mosques. I sat with the women in the mosques, and we chatted and talked. I went to the schools, and I gave talks. I spoke to the staff and the students. Some of them even called me back to speak again. The mayor is seen as the first citizen of the Borough. That means, for example, if the queen were coming to the Borough, she would be the one to first meet and greet the queen. So, I think it was a great honour. I made the most of my mayoral year. As a Deputy Mayor, you only did the extra things that the mayor could not do.

I went to many events; over 500 events in my one year of service as the Mayor. I also managed to raise £44,000 in that one year. I did a lot of activities, and I worked extremely hard because I set a very high standard for myself. Typically, one of the key duties of the mayor was to raise money for their chosen charity, so I chose four charities. One of the charities is Project E18; the brainchild for this project was the former Tottenham footballer Jermaine Defoe. What Project E18 did was to train mentors for young care facility leavers from within the Local Authority aged between 16-19 years. They mentor these young people from care homes in the community as soon as they leave the Local Authority facility that handled the parental responsibilities to these children. Normally, children stay with their parents as long as they want and get real love and care, but with the Local Authority, once the young people are of age, they are free to go and fend for themselves. Unfortunately, some of these young boys may fall into the hands of criminals who could take advantage of them when they go out into the community. So, Jermaine set up this mentoring scheme called Project E18. Some of the money I raised went to them, and that was really nice. They trained some mentors that would mentor the young people when they got out of Local Authority. The young people follow their mentors so they do not get caught up with the pimps and drug barons on the streets, waiting for easy prey to pounce on and get them involved in their criminal activities.

The second charity I raised funds for was the Sickle Cell group in Enfield. The third charity was the Sickle Cell ward at North Middlesex hospital in Enfield where I worked. It was also where I came across women with sickle cell and other people who had the sickle cell disease. I did not just pick sickle cell because it was one of those things people suffer from; it was also because my *mum's nephew died of the sickle cell disease.* So, I wanted to raise funds for sickle cell as well because of my experience. For my fourth charity, I raised funds for "The Voice." The Voice is a small organisation looking after disabled children and their parents in Enfield. They all shared the £44,000 that I raised.

I did a lot of activities to raise money. Enfield is the only Borough that does not have a big council hall for events. As far as I am aware, I was the only mayor who did some of my activities outside the Enfield Borough. I did a sickle cell fundraising party in Selby Centre. At that time, the centre was controlled by the Council and not the private. So, I was charged the charity rate for the hall, which was £700. One of the Nigerian firms in Enfield paid for the hall, so all the other money that I raised was for my charity.

We also hosted a Fun Run that was done on a Saturday in September. We had a Mayor's spring ball as well. I also did another event in my local Catholic Church. I was lucky that the Queen's Jubilee was during my tenure, so I did an event to commemorate that too. There were a lot of other small events as well. I did my service at my local church, St Edmunds. It was massive, and the hall was filled. We were lucky it was during summer when the sun was out. It was beautiful and lovely because I had a lot of people around. The church was jam-packed. We did a magazine as well which was sold on the day. We did anything that we could do to raise funds.

People say they do not know how I did all those things and I did not know too. I think that the Lord is great and that is the only logical explanation I can come up with. One of the things I know about myself is that I am a very determined person. If I say I am going to do something, I will not just do it; I do it well. I also like to do things properly because my dad said to me, "If you are going to do a job, go and do that job properly. And also, 'do for me' is not a good thing. Don't ask people to do things for you."

I had these wise words from my dad at the back of my mind when I did my mayoral role. I had to plan properly. I put together a mayor's committee that met at my house to plan those events. They helped me a lot, planning and executing the functions. The other nice thing about being a mayor was that you were driven in your mayoral car. You were a celebrity for that one year, and it felt good.

I even went to see the Nigerian students in Coventry. I went to The School of Economics under the invitation of the students there. Goldsmiths University which was Goldsmiths College at the time also invited me. I went there to give empowerment talks. I have a profile online, and I think some people might see that and wonder how this woman stays motivated; how she does it all? In Nigeria, people would have said that I bought my degree certificates. But as you all know, you cannot buy certificates in the UK.

Of all my work as a Mayor, I think my favourite part was getting to know the real Enfield where I had spent more than two-thirds of my life. I think it was a great time for me. I did not have any regrets working as a mayor. If I must mention anything, I would probably say that the only regret I have is that I wish I made more money even though a lot of people believe I made a lot more money than other mayors.

To perform my mayoral role properly, I was off work for the whole year. As a councillor, I still maintained my job as most councillors do. As a mayor though, because you had to attend events whenever; morning, afternoon or evening, keeping a job was not realistic. I wanted to raise more money, hence the reason for not continuing with my job at that time.

ROLE OF A COUNCILLOR

As a councillor, you are the mouthpiece of your constituency. The people in the community you live, that is the community you are covering, that is your Ward. You do things like helping get them planning permissions for people who want to build. They have to get approval from the council. Once they submit their plan, the councillors will go through it and visit the area. If it is one that needs consultation with the neighbours, then that has to be done. The neighbours have the right to reject or agree with the plan.

In housing, you want to make sure that the council builds more houses for the residents. However, there is usually not enough money, and without money, you cannot build. This is because the council does not get enough money from the government. From then till now, I do not think the council has built any new homes in Enfield.

And then their health: we work with the hospitals as well as making sure that people's health is adequately monitored.

As for the environment: you have to make sure that there is clean and safe air. This includes things like making sure the bins are taken out. For example, at the moment, there is a consultation out asking if we would prefer our bins being emptied once a week or once every fortnight.

Did I experience any challenges? I am such a positive person that when I try to think about problems, I usually cannot find any. I think the challenge might be trying to juggle my meetings with work because I wanted to do both jobs properly.

Now that I am retired, even though I am no longer on the council at the moment, I am still busy in the political scene. I am the Women Officer, and I am always working to encourage more women, especially ethnic minority women into politics.

I formed an organisation called FAWP (Forum for African, African Caribbean and Asian Women in Politics). It aimed to help with empowering women and equipping them for politics. We launched it on the 3rd of February 2015, and we had an outstanding turnout with over 120 people present.

The Nigerian High Commission sent a representative, Mrs AbdulRazaq who was very impressed with the discussions, the attendants and interest in the organisation. She reported back to the High Commission, and the then High Commissioner Dr Tafida was very impressed too. So much that he wanted to see us. So, I gathered as much of the members as possible, and we went to see him. Dr Tafida said that FAWP was something he had been trying to achieve for some years. He was impressed with what we had, and he was delighted to meet us. He also gave us a donation as well.

I used the opportunity to ask the High Commission that since they were very impressed with what we were doing, if they would become our patron? I am glad they said yes. The organisation has been having meetings on and off and is still going strong till today.

I wear two hats. If I take off the hat of politics, I put on the hat of health care. So, I formed my other organisation in relation to health which is called Tender Care Initiative.

MIDWIFERY

I joined North Middlesex hospital on 8th of May 1972 and left 30th April 2012. I served them for 40 years. This includes three years of my training as a staff nurse and a registered nurse, and eighteen months of training as a midwife. Before then, I worked for one year in the Intensive Care Unit (ICU), so that totals five and a half years. That means that out of forty years, only four years were not in midwifery. I practised midwifery for over 35 years.

I spent all my working life at North Middlesex hospital. It was near where I lived. It was reasonable, and it was no hassle. The hospital had never put any staff on the front cover of their quarterly magazine, but they put me there because of the length of my service and other community achievements. The heading on the magazine was, "From Midwife to Mayor". I thought that it was fantastic. I felt so good. I filled up the whole front page with the interview. There is nothing as good as being nice to people.

In all my 40 years at North Middlesex hospital, I can tell you that not even for one day did I quarrel with anyone. Of course, there were disagreements in the course of our duty. You can go and ask if in doubt. It was a place that I believed showed me how much they cared when I was widowed, and I showed them that I cared about them as well. I gave them 40 years, and they gave me a wonderful send-off via the magazine front page profile. I left when I told them I was going to be a mayor. They could not believe it.

My charities are doing okay. I help out at the children's centre on Wednesdays 10 am -11 am and Thursdays 2 pm

-3 pm. I spend those times helping out women, especially mothers with babies less than one-year-old. I go there, talk with them, ask questions, help them mingle and network. I also try to help them build their self-worth and gain confidence in themselves. Most of them are pregnant and never go out. Doing the things that I do with them helps them and me too. I do not do these things to feel good about myself. I am only impacting what I have learnt and how I feel. I am quite happy that I have been able to do these things.

KEEPING FIT

One might wonder how I manage my energy level with all the activities that I am involved in. I keep up my energy levels by making sure that I keep my body supple and I never allow it to get stiff. I go swimming three times a week, on Mondays but if I cannot make it on Monday because I am babysitting my granddaughter, then l go on Tuesday, Wednesdays and Fridays. I also go to Yoga or Pilates once a week. I have been a full member of Fusion Leisure in Enfield for almost twenty years now. I pay my subscriptions by direct debit and always make sure that I make the most of the payment. I also do some stretches and walking. I walk on Sundays at Albany Park with the Albany Community Walking group. On Fridays, I run a wellbeing exercise group with senior citizens, supported by exercise leaders from Tottenham Hotspur.

ASPIRATIONS

I did not have any more political aspirations after I left the council, but in 2015, there was a vacancy for the Member of Parliament (MP). A lot of people put their names down. I never thought that I would want to be an MP. It was never on my plate at all. My youngest daughter Chinelo kept nagging me saying, "Mummy, put your name down." I said I was not interested. She insisted, "There's nothing in it, if you don't get it, then you don't get it, and you lose nothing." And that was how I decided to put my name down to see if I would get shortlisted.

There were 108 applicants. I thought to myself, with 108 applicants, do I stand a chance? But amazingly, when they were whittled down to twelve, my name was still there. So, I went for the interview on the day. From the twelve, it went down to three, and I was one of them. I could not believe it. Even though I applied, I was still not sure that I wanted to be an MP. I had to listen to my daughter, and as she said, I stood to lose nothing even if I did not get in. I was not keen on the role, but I was pleased that I attempted. This again raised my profile as I was one of the three candidates to be voted for out of 108 and it was fantastic. I may not have won, but it was an achievement for me.

PERSONALITY AND ETHICS

My background or upbringing did not drive my ethics. I think it was inspired by the type of person I grew to become. I want to say that I am self-driven. I am the kind of person who does not like to copy what others do. No. It has to be what I want. I'll not do something simply because someone else is doing it.

I would say I am a strong, determined and assertive person. I am someone with a wealth of knowledge, very humble and respectful to others and I love to level with people. I would also say that I am a person who wants to lead and help others get to where they want to go, especially if it is in an area that I could help.

I want to be remembered as the lady who believed in empowering women and loved to dance. People always ask, "How old is that person?" No, I believe age is a number. I think people should feel instead because the age they feel within their body, is the age they portray. As far as I am concerned, I may be just twenty-five years old today.

One might find it surprising to learn that of all my achievements, I would like to be remembered as the lady who loved to dance.

That said, you will not be surprised to learn that dancing is one of my favourite hobbies, the other being physical health and well-being.

I love to dance. I used to go dancing years and years ago at a dance class in Edmonton Green. I stopped going for too long and then I finally quit. I practised dance moves from the likes of P-Square and D'banj videos on TV.

I love my dancing because nothing is set in stone and nothing lasts forever. As we get older, we lose speed. A time will come when I can no longer do it. While I can, I will have my fill. When the knees are gone, and I can longer do it, I can sit down and watch with happiness and say when I was up there with my feet, and I did all that. Even then, I can still do it in my head. For now though, whenever P-Square comes on, you will always find me on my feet.

AWARDS

I am no stranger to awards, and I have got many of them. It started when I was in secondary school. I got an award because I liked playing netball. Obviously, when our team goes out to play, and we win awards, it is for the whole team members. The way awards were given those days is not the way it is now. I cannot remember any individual awards. It was always like in a group or team of netballers or footballers. These days, I think the winning team gets a trophy, and members of the team get a medal each. I was not good at other sports. There is no sport that I would confidently say I excelled at. But I was very good at netball, and I focused on it. When we win, it is a team effort.

It was when I came to England that awards started flowing. My first recognition was in working as a midwife. I could see people were suffering. I could see people were going through a lot. As a midwife, gradually when you develop a relationship with the mother-to-be, she would then open up and start telling you things. When you hear what some had to say you would soon forget your troubles and complaints because there are people who are worse off than you and I feel a lot of empathy for them.

My work probably helped me get myself into the community. I was doing a lot in the community; working with Enfield Women's Centre that deals with all things women and Enfield Women's Aid that deals with women suffering domestic violence. That was in the nineties. So, I have actually been involved in this Borough for a very long time. So, when I became Councillor I continued with that work.

In April 2007 I was conferred with the **Honorary Freeman of the Borough of Enfield**; this is the highest honour that is conferred on an individual in recognition of their long and valuable service to the Community and their outstanding contribution to the voluntary sector in the Borough.

The title was meaningful in those days; it meant that I could graze my cattle anywhere in the Borough. It also meant I could go into any pub, have a drink and pay nothing. It meant a lot more than I just mentioned. These days it means that you will be invited to any civic event in the Borough. You are on the council's invitation list forever.

I did not know anybody was observant enough and felt I was doing a lot in the community and then nominated me. I was also working with the youths in the community. I just had my tentacles in everything.

As of then, I was bringing up my children and doing my community work. Now that they have all left home, I am doing more in the community than when they were at home. Even then it was still seen as a lot.

Of all my awards, the three most significant ones would be; number one, Honorary Freeman of the Borough. It is not an easy award to get. We can count on our hands how many people have gotten this title. We could even look at the whole of England, and there would just be few.

In Enfield, I do not know how many we are with the title, but I know that on the day that I got mine, there were eight of us, and on that day, I had all my family and friends there. I think the ceremony is done every five years. My number two would be the one I got from Nigeria the Global Power Women Network Africa, and number three would be an award from BEFTA. I have gotten many other awards, of which I am very grateful, but I don't think it is relevant to list all of them.

Maturity includes the recognition that no one is going to see anything in us that we don't see in ourselves. Stop waiting for a producer. Produce yourself.

- Marianne Williamson

Chapter Seven

MY CHILDREN AND ME

I think my children think that mummy is a strong, determined woman and that mummy works very hard.

My siblings love me. They are proud of me as a strong person and as somebody who has always carried them along. I think they have the greatest respect for me because they feel like I've achieved a lot with very little. At times I ask myself what is it that I have achieved; didn't somebody else achieve that as well? I have learnt to not just think of where I want to be, but how far I have come too. It is more like evaluating the options I had in life and thanking God and nature for how far I have come. I have also conditioned my mind and body for the days ahead.

Raising my children alone was not easy. Naturally, I am somebody who believes in success. I never thought that I could fail and I have developed the attitude to get things to work. I have got two boys and two girls and no man in the house. Each boy is different from the other. I will tell you about the easy one first - my younger son, Chukwuma. I'll probably say he is more like an angel. He is not someone who likes to hang about outside. He is a stay at home type of person. So, I think I was fortunate that after school, he comes back and stays indoors except when he had football or any of the other extracurricular activities.

My older son Amaechi likes going out. Going out was not the problem; it was the people who you mix with when you are out. I remember saying to him one day – which is true- because when my husband was alive, we had always discussed the children attending secondary school back in Nigeria. So, as soon as I saw the kind of friends he was keeping, I reminded him about that. You know it could be challenging with the boys. Fortunately, I had good family friends. So, what I did was to engage with one of them. I said to them please can you talk to my son about mixing with other young boys. Mind you, the youths in those days were not as challenging as we have these days. There was nothing like gang business in those days. I was lucky in that aspect, but I was still eager to send him home.

I was pleased that my brothers were there and handy as his role models in Nigeria. He got particularly close to my brother, Arinze. By doing that, I had fulfilled my agreement with my husband. This was so that he could pick up the responsibilities of being the eldest son, get to know our culture, pick up the language and probably even help him become a better person. It was quite easy to do because one of my close friends lived in Enugu State as of then. She and her husband were eager to offer some assistance. I met the lady when we were in Adazi, Anambra State during our teacher's training and we had become very close friends. After her training, she got married and ended up here in London. When I came to London, we met up and continued being close since we were already friends from Nigeria.

The couple were from Nimo in Anambra State, and they were also the godparents of my eldest daughter. In those days, when people accomplished what they wanted to in London, they headed back to Nigeria. They were one of those who decided to go back to Nigeria. The lady was teaching at the Federal Government College, Enugu. This made it easy for me to arrange for Amaechi, my eldest son to attend secondary school there. He had already attended one year here in London at St Ignatius RC Secondary School in Borough of Enfield here. He was happy to go because it was something that I had always drummed into his ears. This was also something I had discussed with his daddy, and he probably would have wanted him to carry on and do it especially since it would help him to learn about our culture.

In a way, it was like a swap deal because they wanted their daughter who was the same age as Amaechi to come and study for her secondary education in London. Their daughter came to live with me and Amaechi went to live with them.

Amaechi lived with them for five years, which was the length of his secondary school. He came to London every single holiday as long as it was up to a week because that was my promise to him. Amaechi came to London for holidays twice a year, and I went to Nigeria once a year for five years. I also made sure that he lacked nothing. I bought every single thing that I thought he liked and used and I filled a trunk box in my living room with all those things. I also loaded stuff like tea, coffee, washing up liquid, sweets, toothbrush, toothpaste, cereals, tablets of nice soaps, all little essentials and goodies; you name it, I had it in the trunk box, and also something for my friend. It was quite easy for me to fill up. If I go to the shop and see something on sale or some other thing that I knew he liked, I would buy them, and I kept doing that until the box got full.

It might seem like I spent more money on Amaechi during this period than on his siblings, but no I did not. My other children did not need extra expenditure because they were still young. My eldest daughter had a university grant, so I did not spend much on her too because of that. So, Amaechi was the only child I needed to spend on. The nice thing about him coming to London twice a year was that he kept in touch with his friends and siblings. This way, it did not feel like I kept him away from his siblings or a lingering feeling that his mum and dad were not there.

He liked it in Nigeria. He made good friends there and settled in very well while facing his studies. Those things that I bought and stored in the trunk box were taken care of by a family friend. The family friend travels in and out and exports items to Nigeria. So, once my trunk box was ready, he would freight it to Nigeria, and I just paid the cost of freight. The contents of the box lasted long for them, and they never lacked. Everything I put in the box was for the whole family, not just my son. They were things they could also use in the house. With my son there, they were like my extended family. We did things together. Ever since the war, I used to visit my friend Cecilia in Nimo, Anambra State, so we came from way back.

There is something about Nimo I have always believed that if I were not engaged or tied down at an early age, I would have liked to live in Nimo because that was where all my friends came from. Even my childhood friend from when we lived in Jos was also from Nimo. During the war, my best friend was from Nimo, and coming over to the UK coincidentally again, my other best friend whom I met at work in North Middlesex hospital was also from Nimo. My life circled around Nimo, and I believe that was where I could have been married into because I made friends from there since I was in the North, then the East and also here in London. It is unbelievable, and I cannot see how such a coincidence could happen. It is a kind of one in a million chances that your three best friends were all from the same place. I still remain very close to those three best friends of mine.

Sending my son to Nigeria was not really because his behaviour was that of a bad child, but because I felt that my son was growing and being the eldest, I thought I had to fulfil the arrangement I had with my husband. We agreed that all the children would attend secondary school in Nigeria. Even if he did not associate with friends I did not approve of, I would have still sent him to Nigeria, so I could fulfil the agreement.

Didi was in her first year in secondary school when my husband passed away. I decided to allow her to complete her secondary school here in London and then attend university in Nigeria instead. She was also quite happy to go to university in Nigeria, but the only thing in Nigeria that was not very good was that the universities were always on strike. She went to the University of Nigeria, Nsukka in Enugu state where she studied Law.

When my eldest son completed his secondary education, he came back to London for a two-year A-Levels at St Ignatius RC College. After his A-Levels, he started applying to universities because he wanted to study Arts which he was very good at. I believe he got the genes from my husband who was a designer. Amaechi was also outstanding in Fine Arts. He gained admission for a one-year Foundation course at Middlesex University, and he liked it. He later moved on for his three-year degree, studying Fine Arts. Because Middlesex University was in Enfield where we lived, he travelled from home. As of that time, he was qualified for the government grant that covered their tuition fee and travel expenses.

At this time, Didi who was in Nigeria spent only eighteen months due to the constant strike. She was becoming unhappy, and I was unhappy as well. Whenever she came to London on holiday and saw her friends whom they got into the university at about the same time as her leaving her behind, she got upset. I was also concerned too because she was stuck in her first year due to university strikes in Nigeria while her mates were in their second year. Then we mutually agreed that it was time for her to come back because it was not worth wasting her time over. She was quite happy about coming back to London.

When she came back, she got admission into Southampton University and for some reason; maybe because she was away from home, she did not like it very much even though we went to visit her regularly. So, she transferred to Thames Valley University in Ealing and lived on the campus.

My two youngest children did not go to school in Nigeria because by now, I was not impressed with the education system in Nigeria. It had changed from what it used to be. Although, I would have loved for them to attend, especially the secondary education, but my friend and I agreed that the younger ones might as well carry on with their secondary education in London.

As I mentioned earlier, my youngest son Chukwuma is very quiet; he is not what you might call streetwise. He is a good disciplinarian himself and a home person; that is who he is. All he wanted was to go to school, come back home and stay indoors. If he wanted to go out, he would go with only a few friends. He never got the street cred. He carried on with his secondary school at St Ignatius RC. When he finished, again he applied to universities and got a place at the University of Hertfordshire. The travel was easy, so he went from home. He studied Business and Economics. After he finished university, he did not want to go further. As much as I would have loved for him to study for his Master's degree; however, he was old enough to know what he wanted. He later got a job working with an agency and from there got a fulltime job that he is still at with the Ministry of Immigration.

Chinelo, whom I call my handbag did not school in Nigeria as well. I think it was particularly difficult for me to send her to Nigeria because it was like we were attached at the waist. I call her my handbag, my princess and mummy's other half. We are very close, maybe it was because she was only eighteen months old when her dad passed away, and I was the only parent she ever knew or perhaps because she was just the youngest; I do not know, but we are very close. She also went to a Catholic Secondary school called St Ann's RC which was an all-girls school.

My two boys went to St Ignatius RC which was a boys school, and my two girls went to St Ann's.

My children were all aware of the importance of education and what it meant for their future. They all studied very hard and gained good degrees at the University. My eldest daughter Didi is very intelligent. My youngest daughter is also intelligent but not as much as her elder sister. She can be a very determined person though. When she wants something, she aims at getting it, and she gets it. I remember when she was in the University, she told me she intended to make a 2:1 in her degree, and being a determined person, she worked hard and achieved her desired degree. She studied Media Technology at Kingston University.

What I did for all my children was to pay for them to have extra-tutorial at home in the subject they felt they needed to improve on. I was very determined for my children to succeed education wise. This helped them and also helped me to make sure that I helped them to achieve academically.

Didi studied Law which was what I wanted, but it was never what she wanted. Later on, I realised I had to let my children study what they wanted else, I would be like my parents. So, I had to let go, and I was more relaxed with other children after the first. Chinelo did very well in her secondary school and university. We were so close that when she went to the university, I was hoping and praying that she would settle quickly because I wanted her to live out of the house so she could start mixing with others and start developing her own identity. She wanted to go to Middlesex University which was very close to home. Inside me, I did not want her to travel from home; I prayed for her to detach from me and attend a university where she could live on the campus so that she would be able to cope without her mum.

Fortunately for me, the course she wanted to study, she found in Kingston University which was good because she could now live away from home, but also close enough for her to easily come home. She came home almost every week. If she comes and I was not there, she did not mind as long as she was home, she could feel my presence. Sometimes, she came while I was at work because she did not know my shift. The only way I knew she had been home was if I went into the kitchen and I found the food ladder and fridge empty. She came home whenever she wanted, be it a weekday or a weekend to get foodstuff.

All my children had a particular thing that I did for each of them. For Chinelo, in her first year, she lived in a self-contained accommodation. She was one of the few students who had self-contained accommodation. All she shared was the kitchen. She had an en-suite shower. I bought her a fridge-freezer which was kept in her room, and I was pleased with that. By the time she finished her first year, she had made some good friends. In her second year, she and her friends rented and shared a house. That helped her to settle.

It was very hard the first day that her siblings and I drove her to the university. We were all crying even though she was still in London. If I behaved that way while she was in London, I wonder how I would have acted if I had to send her to Nigeria. It would have been tough for me to send her to Nigeria because of our close relationship.

PERSONAL RELATIONSHIP WITH MY CHILDREN

My relationship with all my children is varied. With Chinelo as mentioned earlier, we have always been very close. With Chukwuma, it is good. With Amaechi, it is quite good as well because one thing about him up till today is he is very respectful of me. It is a nice thing because I think at long last, although there was no argument about going to Nigeria, he found that it helped him a lot in becoming the man he is, and it helped him develop better relationships. With Didi, my relationship was not as close as with others, and I think it was because being the eldest, I was stricter on her to make sure we did things right. It was like climbing some stairs. You are careful about the first steps because if you miss them, you might fall over. I did not want to get it wrong with my children. I think at times she was not too pleased with my treatment of her. But being a girl, I was afraid she would show up unexpectedly with some pregnancy. I was mindful of the hours she went out and the time she had to get back in.

There may have been some resentment about that, and even while Chinelo was growing, she sometimes compared them and accused me of allowing Chinelo to stay out longer than she used to. In return, I would say to her that with her, I was learning to be a parent and not because I was closer to Chinelo. I let her know those times were never to punish her. I explained to her that reason why I asked her to come back home at 10 pm was because I was being careful, and I did not want her to stay out until midnight and cause me to panic. Chinelo did not stay out that much later, but she happened to go out more often. I think that she did not like this very much. She must have felt that I liked Chinelo more. For me, I believe I gave them equal care and love.

I spent a lot of money on Didi as well, because during the eighteen months she spent in Nigeria, she was also coming to London regularly. When she came back to resettle, I got her extra tutorials, and I spent a lot on that. She went to Holborn College for her extra tutorial, and it was quite expensive. She attended during the weekends.

Now my relationship with Didi, I think it's like that of two good friends. I would also describe it as that of two adults who would sit down to talk about themselves rather than interfering. I do not interfere with her at all. Neither do I with the boys. I let them do what adults should do. She is a career person who loves her job. It is funny with my children; the two youngest are married while the two eldest are not married at present. I think what I like to remember most about my children is that I was able to bring all of them up without any of them getting into trouble. Plus, they all went to university. It is not that if you do not go to university, you have failed; it was just what I had hoped and prayed for. I did not want one to attend while others did not because they might come back later to ask, "How come I didn't go to university!" You know with children even if it is their fault, they always blame their parents, and that was why I had to put extra money for them to get extra-tutorials.

With integrity, you have nothing to fear, since you have nothing to hide. With integrity, you will do the right thing, so you will have no guilt.

-Zig Ziglar

Chapter Eight

COPING WITH FINANCES

With finances, I was very fortunate because our house was not of a high mortgage as it was purchased in the eighties. With my midwifery profession, by 1984 I was already at the peak of my career. In 1985, I became a midwifery sister before my husband passed away. I went up my career ladder very quickly. Fortunately for nurses, we had the opportunity to do agency work. I did agency work which was extra earnings for the extra things I was doing for the children.

I worked at North Middlesex hospital during the week and did agency over the weekend. This could be just a Friday night shift for the agency work. That one shift was enough, but I also did it regularly. It could be used to pay my bills, the extra tutorials or the children's school outings. The children never missed any school outings.

The children never missed any get-together or outing. If you were to ask them, they would tell you that their mum was always out there with them anywhere they went. You see the parties I go to now, I used to go with them. As they grew up, they pulled themselves out. We used to go to parties and come back at 3 am or 4 am in the morning. The children were never on left alone; there was always someone looking after them.

Amongst themselves, they did not fight, but they had arguments. Their arguments were mostly over house chores. On Saturdays, each of them had their chores. One of them was in charge of cleaning the fridge. The person had to take everything out of the fridge, clean it and put everything back inside. One of them was in charge of hoovering the whole house. One of them was in charge of putting all the washing in the washing machine to wash and then somebody was in charge of ironing. The chores rotated monthly. The argument would be when someone tells the other, "You were supposed to be hoovering, but you did not hoover the house properly." The person would reply, "But I did" and the other person would say, "But look at this corner." Then I would be called, "Mummy, come, Amaechi or whoever's turn it was, did not do the hoovering properly". Then I would go and tell the person, "it is true you didn't do it properly." Now when it was the turn of the person who was complained against, they would retaliate and lodge a similar complaint. These were the kinds of arguments that they had.

TALKING ABOUT THEIR DAD

We talked about their dad whenever we wanted. We made sure that during the anniversary of his passing, we say a Mass and we did that regularly. I do that on my own these days, and I remind them. I do not want to take their lives from them because they are adults now. I leave them to do what they want to do. To tell you honestly, I played that part of mother and father by making sure they lacked nothing. As for toys, they got those. None of them had to miss school because there was no money to pay. I took them out shopping. At times they could see that they had more things than some children from two-parent homes.

EMOTIONAL DISCIPLINE

I was extremely involved in the community, and I don't even know how the community aspect evolved. It was like an eruption. I found myself working in the community. I got involved in Enfield Women's Aid because I met a lot of women in my line of work who were experiencing domestic violence. I cannot tell how I worked myself into that, but there I was with them, having meetings and so forth. I let the children know what mummy was doing. Whenever I went to meetings, I told them where I was going to, and they usually had their things to do too. When they wanted to go out, I let them go with their friends and sometimes we would go together.

Sometimes they might want to go to the cinema. Every time there was a new film out for children, I made sure they always went. They went with their school friends, and we also went with their parents as well, and this was how I also made some other friends. How this happened was if the children wanted to see a film with their school friends, and because they needed to be accompanied by adults, I would request for other mums to join us too. Or we arranged with them when we meet at their school for a convenient weekend when we all met up at the cinema to see the film together. Sometimes, we took the children to the seaside.

I was a busy mother doing the things that I like to do but at the same time making sure that my children never missed out on anything. So, weekends at times we went bike riding, or we went to the park. We went to the park a lot. Whenever I was not at work, I was with the children.

POLITICAL CAREER STARTING

I became a Councillor when the children had all grown in 2002. But I got actively involved in politics when I finished my Law degree in 1997.

I studied for my law degree from 1992 to 1997. My general nursing was from May 1972 to May 1975. After I qualified as a Registered Nurse, I worked in the Intensive Care Unit for one year, before commencing a one-year Midwifery Training and qualified in 1977. Then I started working full time as a midwife.

All my nursing and midwifery studies and work was at North Middlesex hospital, and that is why I have a soft spot for the hospital. I should have considered owning shares in the hospital. I chuckle at this thought whenever it crosses my mind. I met and nursed many pregnant women who had Sickle Cell Blood Disorder. Hence, I chose the Sickle Cell and Thalassaemia Unit, North Middlesex University Hospital as one of the Mayor's charity. At the end of my Mayoral year, out of £44,000 that I raised, I donated £15,000 to the Unit. The money was invested towards the purchase of equipment, and on the 24th of November 2016, I was invited for the ribbon cutting ceremony to launch the equipment which I think was very nice. This was the bulk of the money I raised. Nobody else had donated such amount to the unit. I am very passionate about Sickle Cell Blood Disorder, and I will continue to support the unit until the Blood Exchange Machine is purchased.

I loved the general nursing practice. When I was doing my midwifery training, I had the intention of going back to general nursing. I just wanted to do midwifery for the additional certificate. But by the time I finished my midwifery training, I discovered it was a wonderful profession. Being a midwife was such an honour. To help bring a human into the world was amazing and that was what kept me there even after I finished my Law degree. Although, I mentioned that I had a hindrance concerning that because of the cost of the School of Law tuition of £7000 in conjunction with my mortgage.

Inasmuch I achieved what I achieved, I think one of my regrets was not being able to pay the £7000 for the Law school to enable me to practice Law. I could not do it part-time either because I was still required to put down a huge deposit.

I believe I coped very well while studying part-time for my Law degree but I had to cut down my outings such as attending parties. The parties were not as bad as it is now, although there were not a lot of parties then compared to now. I made sure that the extra time I had was for the children. The children saw me studying, so they were able to do more of their homework because I was always studying. Then seeing mummy who was already an adult studying, they thought that studying must be very good. I became their role model in that sense.

My children were very obedient, and it was because I never had to be harsh on them. I was a mother to them. I never brought them up with heavy hand. At times, I was able to sense the kind of friend or company they kept, and I would say to them, "You see that your friend, I don't think he or she is a very nice person. They hang around, or they do this, or they do that. If they ask you to accompany them to any place, don't go; because sometimes you don't know where they're taking you to." I would say things like these to them, and they usually listened.

COMMUNITY WORK BEFORE JOINING THE COUNCIL

I was very much involved in the church. I think the church was one of the places that helped me a lot with the children because they were brought up as Catholics so attending church every Sunday became a part of them. Also, in the Catholic Church, we have Mass Servers and Catechists. The Catechists help the children prepare for Holy Communion or Confirmation. So, my children got involved in those roles. My eldest daughter was a Catechist while the younger ones were Mass Servers. That helped in moulding them and in keeping them as Christians. It formed the basis of their moral standards. It also helped them in being respectful to parents and other people.

I was very much involved in the community. Like I said earlier, my midwifery helped me to find that there was a domestic violence group where I assisted in supporting the women who had come to them for help and advice. Working with my children also showed me that young people also needed support. So, I got involved with young people. I got involved with the young people because I had developed a soft spot for them from when I studied with them while working on my Law degree.

As a mature student with four children, I was made to form a study group with young people. Funny enough they loved studying with me. There is one thing I'm very particular about, and that is when we plan to meet; we must meet dead on time. If somebody is missing, I am always on the lookout. When the person shows up next time, I will rebuke him or her by saying, "Where did you go? You didn't come for the study group the other day?" They would make a joke and say, "Oh my goodness, I got away to university and lived out of home to have time to myself and get away from my mother, but look now, this one is even worse than our mother." We would all laugh about it, and afterwards, there would be no hard feelings.

One thing I made sure of was for them to know the boundary. That was why I decided they had to call me "Aunty Kate." So, I being called Aunty Kate did not start today, it started a long time ago because I always got involved with much younger people. Even the young mothers who were my close friends and much older than the young people called me Aunty Kate as well. I cannot tell why, but for some reason, I tend to get on extremely well with young people, young mothers and young families. Somehow my attitude towards them makes them come closer to me. I also had a lot of them who wanted some advice and mentoring from me.

ENFIELD WOMEN'S AID

I met the young mothers and young families from my work as a community midwife and in Enfield Women's Aid. We held the organisation meetings, and in the meetings, we always had a trustee present. In the meetings, we typically discussed a new baby and mother or about a woman on her own. Where necessary, we help to find refuge places for them outside the Borough. This was to make sure the perpetrator did not know where his victim lived. I helped out as a volunteer as it had nothing to do with my midwifery, although I learnt about them from my work as a midwife. When they told me their problems during the course of my midwifery work, I sought out organisations to signpost them to, and that was how I found Enfield Women's Aid.

I joined Enfield Women's Aid as a trustee, and there I learnt a lot of refuge addresses where the women could go. So, when I come across the women who need the services in my midwifery, I tell them where to phone and what advice they can get etc.

We had trustee meetings once a month. In the meetings, we also discussed activities for the women and organisation. We did activities such as confidence building as well as go to outings with them. In addition, we did fundraising activities and conferences where we invited other people to attend and support the organisation. So, the things that I am doing now were things that I learnt years and years ago.

Apart from the Enfield Women's Aid, I also volunteered for The Youth Centre in Edmonton which was another community group. We worked with young people in the centre and encouraged them. They came for activities because young people liked active fun, so at Henlon Youth Centre where I helped out, we planned and went on outings to the seaside, cinema or Theme Parks. Inside the centre, they had exercise machines and a manager who ran it. We liaised with the manager to know the number of people attending and from where. Some of them came from difficult backgrounds with mental health issues, so we had activities to keep them active.

I also got myself into Enfield Law centre. At this centre too, we had trustees. We also had the Citizens Advice Bureau (CAB) where people went for advice. For those who needed legal counsel and the waiting time was too long at CAB; we at the Enfield Law Centre arranged for qualified lawyers to give pro-bono advice to people with immigration problems, council tax arrears and financial problems to know how they could organise a payment plan. I helped out there to make sure I utilised my knowledge of the law.

MOTIVATION TO BECOMING A COUNCILLOR

My motivation for becoming a Councillor was because the women I attended at ante- and post-natal always had questions to ask. They had housing problems; they probably had immigration and financial issues too. Some of them were not able to pay their council tax, or maybe the council said they owed them and they did not know how it came about, and they had been trying to get a hold of somebody to speak to but were having difficulty. Or maybe in the neighbourhood where they lived, they had noise from neighbours etc.

When I went to see them as a midwife, they told me their problems, but they did not know who to ask for help. Sometimes, they say that they had called their council because people told them to call but no one answered, or when they got an answer, they were asked to call back later. The only way I believe in finding solutions for them was to go to the council myself because they had difficulty getting to them. It was easier for me to make enquiries. I could walk into the place and say, "oh, I'm a midwife with so and so, I wonder if it's possible to see someone from the housing department." It was easier than the client going. So, I found that I was succeeding and I asked myself how these people called Councillors whom I went to ask, how they got there.

It was through that that I was motivated to say I would like to be a Councillor. I found out that to be one you have to be affiliated to a political party. By this time, I was already going to political party meetings, but I did not know that it would lead me to become a Councillor.

I think I picked my party of choice by listening to things that were happening and I found that the Labour Party always talked about the ethnic minority, the poor and single parents. So, I thought this party is the kind party that cares about the poor people, and these are the values that I admired and liked. I felt the Conservative Party seemed to be all rich people and I wondered if they would be able to look after the poor. It may sound funny, and I am not sure if other people had the same thought, but that was how I got into the Labour party. These days, when people ask me, I tell them I like the Labour party because they had all the values that I admired and I wanted to be part of them.

Then I made enquiries to find out where the Labour Party office was, and when I got there, they asked me to fill out a form and pay a small subscription fee to become a member of the party. They then told me when they had their meetings. So, I started attending their meetings. At the meetings, I usually sit at the back, not knowing or contributing to what they were talking about.

When my children were in school, I kept hearing about school governor, but I did not understand it. When I realised what a school governor was, I thought to myself, how come nobody explained this to me earlier. I would have loved to become one. When I become a school governor, I said to myself, this is what I should have been doing a long time. Not that I would have given up the Women's Aid because school governor was also voluntary. But I was happy that I found out and I have been a school governor till now, and that has been over 15 years.

I started with one school called Cuckoohall Lane Primary School. I was a school governor there for only a short period, however. While a school governor there, I continued attending Labour Party meetings and I found that there were primary schools close to our meeting venue. The primary schools were also very close to where I lived, so I asked myself how come I was going to Cuckoohall Lane Primary School when Raynham Primary School and

Wilbury Primary School were opposite North Middlesex hospital where I worked. These schools were just about ten minutes walk away. So, I decided to join the nearest two to me. I was quite happy that I joined two of them and I am still there up till now.

At the Labour party meetings, they talked about elections coming up in 2002, and at this time I still felt like I was not sure of what I was doing. One thing that I liked doing was going to conferences. So, when there was a conference, I always put my hand up to attend, whether it was the women's or Labour Party conference. Then I participated in a conference with our then Member of Parliament (MP) for Edmonton Andy Love. When we got there, he introduced me to one of the MPs, and he said to the MP, "Oh this is Councillor Kate Anolue." I quickly corrected him by saying that I was not a councillor. He said, "But you'll be." I said okay, but when the time was right, not now. He said to the MP, "Don't mind her; she's outstanding." Many other members of the party went to the conference, but the Edmonton branch sponsored me.

I remember when the forms were out; you could self-nominate or people could nominate you for councillorship. MP Andy Love said to me, "Get a form, you'll be good at the council." I said no, not yet, maybe next time. Andy Love helped by encouraging me, and he said, "No, no, no you must fill up the form now." So, I picked up the self-nomination form, and that was how the story started.

I completed the form and was lucky to be shortlisted. The selection was more difficult, with a lot of campaigning and lobbying members of the Ward for their votes. Eventually, I was selected. Then we started working hard to be elected on the Election Day. But because we had always worked with Andy Love's campaigns, we already knew how to campaign. So, I campaigned. I checked, and there were not many people from ethnic minorities. As I campaigned, I also encouraged people from the ethnic minority to join the party. I was also the Ethnic Minority Officer, and that helped me to work and encourage people from ethnic minorities to become active in politics. Also, when I became the Women Officer, I concentrated on women, and as time went on, I was able to encourage more women to join. I campaigned, and I was successful.

I was first elected as Councillor for Upper Edmonton in 2002, re-elected in 2006, and again in 2010. So, I was a Councillor for twelve years.

I got quite involved in other activities, and with my midwifery knowledge, I give talks in the schools, sometimes when they have things like their baby week. I go to give talks about how to handle babies and giving baby bath demonstration to the children. I did that whenever they needed me, and I enjoyed that.

Lots of people want to ride with you in the limo, but what you want is someone who will take the bus with you when the limo breaks down.

-Oprah Winfrey

Chapter Nine

COMMUNITY ENGAGEMENT ACTIVITIES

WIDOWS AND ORPHANS

I do not know how I got involved with the activities of widows and orphans, but I believe that because so much had happened in my life that looking back, I feel that I had every reason to empathise with widows. I think it all started with my own experience. I know that back at home, in the Igbo land there were cultures and customs. Many of them demeaned women. For me, those ones treated women as if they were lesser human beings. One of those 'cultures' is widowhood. I am talking from experience because I was widowed over thirty years ago here in England.

When I became a widow, my children were eighteen months old, five, nine and twelve years old respectively. The thing I was most concerned about was bringing up the children on my own. However, I did not know there was more to come when we got home to Nigeria for my husband's burial. There was something my husband and I believed in, and that was that our final resting place had to be in Nigeria. I am happy that I fulfilled that for my husband. I was brought up in Nigeria, and I would like to rest in Nigeria too.

So, we got back home. There was something silly about the tradition of the Igbo in those days with regards to a woman and the corpse of her husband. The tradition stated that a woman must not see the body or the remains of her husband because it was an abomination. I saw him at the undertakers' here in London and I shed my tears and all that. I believe that counts as me seeing his corpse. However, I was told that whatever happened in England was irrelevant. I could not believe it. I had heard about that before so it was not like it was new to me, but I still could not believe it. I felt that since I had already seen his body in London that would nullify whatever they said, but no. That was a big problem for me because it meant that if I did not see my husband's body in front of the rest of the community and he was buried, that means..., I feel so bad telling you now because it feels so heavy on my tongue. That means that any of his male relatives could walk into my house and get into bed with me, and I had no right to say no.

I looked at it and for me, a highly educated person coming from England, after my general nursing and midwifery, working full time only to go home and behave like a pagan; I totally refused. So, I realised I had a job to do, and it was that I had to see the remains of my husband in front of his relatives before he was buried. If I did not do that, I was going to be almost a slave to the men. I would be their punch bag for their sexual satisfaction to be explicit.

So, what I did was, I spoke with my immediate younger brother. I asked him about the burial procedure. He said, "Well in the morning of the day of the burial, the coffin would be opened. My husband's sister and family members would come to cry over it, and that was the only time it was going to be opened. After that, it would be closed, and that was it." I said to my brother, no matter what you do; make sure that you alert me when they open the coffin. He told me it would be around 4 am. I said no problem; I did night duties back in England so being awake by that time was very easy for me. So, he stayed over.

In the morning around 3 am, I was already awake. As the widow, you had a special chair where you sit. So, I sat there. I had a very dear friend who used to live in England but had relocated and was now working at Owerri University Hospital in Nigeria at that time. She came and stayed with me. So, on the said night until the following morning, I sat on the bench with her. I saw my brother pacing up and down, and he made a sign to me that it was getting close to the time. Then I heard footsteps coming, and the minute they were opening the casket, my brother gave me a sign. I had never been so brisk or eager in my life. For me, it was going to be the beginning or the end of me. I did tell my brother that if I failed to see the corpse in front of his family, I would run to England and never come back to Nigeria.

So, as soon as the casket was opened, he called me, and I rushed in with such speed like my life depended on it. My late husband's relatives were unaware of what was happening when they opened the casket. I immediately buried my head into the casket as they were trying to close it. I said to the remains of my husband, "I know you'll never let this happen to me. I know you'll never let anybody play football with me or use me any way they liked."

They thought that they could walk into the house and grab everything. Although we did not have much, it seemed like all he had belonged to his immediate brothers. The unfortunate thing was that none of them thought about the children or the widow of the dead man. All they thought about was his property, enslaving and using his widow as the punching bag for their frustrations and sexual satisfaction.

You should have seen their reaction when I buried my head in the casket. I always have a full smile whenever I remember it. Before you could say, Jack Robinson, the story had gone all over the town and people were saying, "Wise woman from England. I heard she's seen her dead husband's body. Doesn't she know that it's a way of saying I don't want you men to come near me? So, who's going to help her look after her children or do the things she wants like climbing to get palm nuts and all those jobs that men would do etc."

For God's sake, who needs all this? Who told them that I was going to be living in the village? Even if I was there in the village, I am an educated woman with two certificates, my general nursing and midwifery. I think there is always a level that one is above. I am above that manipulative paganism and the selfish attitude of those men.

Once that was done, they almost left the corpse. They ran out horrified, and they cried what an awful abomination I had committed. They said, "Don't worry she'll be dead in the next one year." But I am still here, and it has been over thirty years now.

One thing they refused to do was to shave my hair which was the normal thing to do when someone's husband passed away. Immediately the corpse was buried, your hair would be, and it was your husband's family's duty to do that. But did we care? My cousins, sister and brothers were there. In fact, they were ready to shave my hair as soon as the burial was done. In the evening they shaved my hair, and we wrapped the hair and took them back to my father's compound because you never know what those people are up to.

That was done, and then I had to wear black clothes which were the norm again. But these days women tend to wear white. The most essential part now was sitting out on a mat in front of the veranda which I did. Every morning by 5 am, you made sure you had washed and eaten, and you would go to sit there. My sister and cousins cooked food in our house and brought to me at my husband's place because I married in the same village, so our house was quite close.

I had to sit for I think ten days or so, I do not quite remember because it was done by market days. You sat there all day. You only got up for toilet breaks and to go and eat. You sat there, and people would come to pay their respects and condolence visits. I thought it was very demeaning for the woman. People can sit with you. My friend and my sister sat with me. They swapped because it was very tedious. You did not speak much in this period. People come to greet you, and you could not shake anyone's hand. Sometimes, people came with condolence gifts and money. You could not touch those either. There was a tray beside you, and they put the items there. The widow does not touch anything; when inside the house you could but not outside. This carried on for the entire period.

I went home with my three children. Fortunately, we had a wonderful lady as a childminder whom I would probably call my elder sister except that she was white (anyone would see through that). She was that good to us, but she has passed on now. We called her Aunty Pearl. May her soul rest in peace. They were a lovely family. She had two boys and one girl. She was childminding full-time, so she picked my children from school. While I was in Nigeria, she looked after my eighteen-month-old baby in England, so I was able to travel with the other three.

We stayed for the important initial days that I was supposed to be sitting. Immediately after that, we came back to England.

Because I saw my husband's remains his family were very bitter about it, especially his sister. He had one sister. I think he had a younger brother whom I think I am older than. I still cannot understand if it was my husband's rascal younger brother who they planned to pass me on to. His sister kept malice with me because I saw my husband's remains, and the feeling was mutual because as far as I was concerned, I was protecting myself and the interests of my children. Nobody from the family cared about my children. All they were after was my body probably. Like our people say, "One is above certain things." And I know with my profession, I would be able to look after my children. It would take some sacrifices, but I prefer that.

I think this was where my interest in widows and vulnerable women kicked in because I asked myself the question; "Does it mean that if I wasn't educated, that was the treatment that I would have received?" That is the treatment women are getting up till today, thirty years on. Although in my village, things have changed, a lot of women went through hell to effect this change. However, the change is very significant.

The thing that has changed was the belief that a widow did not have the right to see her husband's corpse in front of his family. Why should a widow run away from the body of her husband when he's dead? The same woman who was with him for donkey years or even if it was one year? Why should people stop her from seeing the body? That has changed. Occasionally, you still get those misogynistic men or whatever term is right for them who still practice such 'culture'. Children, with their education and enlightenment, would not sit and watch their mum get maltreated. It still happens till this day in some places, however.

There are places where women do not have land and do not have access to their husband's properties either. These are the reasons why women should be educated.

I owe my dad so much. I am one of seven children; two girls and five boys. His friends told him several times not to educate me because I would get married and then my education would be a waste of money. I look back now and wonder what would have become of me if I did not get any education. I would probably still be in the village, and my children would suffer because they would be begging for school fees from whoever had agreed to support them in school and higher education.

I do not know what would have happened, but I know very well that nothing else got me where I am today if not education. With education, I was wise, and I was empowered. People say that knowledge is power. It is not just power; it empowers you to be able to think straight. To think about your rights, and think about the things you want to do for yourself and for your children, and how you want to progress in the world economy. Without it, you could not think that far. Majority of the women that I have seen even till now are those women who did not have much education or who have not been exposed to much. Some are educated, but they have men telling them that they could be seen and never to be heard; that their place was in the kitchen.

We cannot let this continue because I believe that when God created us human beings. He created man and woman. He did not create only Adam, and neither did He create only Eve. Each one was created to support the other. In Igbo land we say "*Akannikwo aka ekpe, aka ekpeakwo aka nni*" meaning "If the left hand washes the right hand, the right hand will wash the left hand." If you look at it, when you are washing your hands they are interlocking.

You can never wash your hands properly if you decided to wash only your right or left hand. To wash your hands properly, it means you have got to get the two of them to work together. The left and right are like marriage. They are entangled.

I believe that education allows women to expand their knowledge. Education does not mean that you have to go to university. Education means getting the basic knowledge you need to survive in life because not all of us in this world are going to be academicians. Some people are very artistic and skilled. However, they need that primary education to empower them to be able to ask questions and to fashion themselves and their minds to what they want to do. With only that basic education, they can get a lot of things done.

I have listened to women who are going through domestic violence while working as a midwife, so I know where they are coming from. I was their listening ears and the shoulder they cried on.

TENDER CARE HEALTH INITIATIVE

I started running the Tender Care Health Initiative because of my interest in working with women in the community. Following my bereavement and return to work, I was always thinking about widows, and this led me to think about women in general. If a woman is widowed and she is not educated, she would be quite happy to be looked after by her husband's siblings or anyone within the family as long as they told her they could help her raise the children and do other things. Before you become a widow, certain things should have been in place. If those things are missing, and you become a widow, you will suffer. And that is why I continue to talk about education. It is fine to say that; however, she would still be oppressed because she cannot do things for herself.

My work is education. We need to get people into school. I usually work with women and organise conferences. Majority of the conferences teach women about; firstly, to thank God for every sex of children we have. Some people think that you must have boys. They believe that only male children matter. So, that means that girls are already destined to suffer from birth because if you were to ask a man what his wife had, most would say, "Oh she had a girl." It is like it is nothing. And that is how women maltreatment starts.

Secondly, we have to appreciate the girl child. When we appreciate the girl child, we have an open mind to their education. My work is working with women to talk about education. It is not merely working with widows. You have to work with every woman to enlighten them. If they have a girl child, they should make sure that she goes to school. You must tell them that by so doing they will be able to help themselves. This way they do not have to live their lives on handoffs. When the person who gives you is no longer around, then you suffer. So, you want to let them know that they need to broaden the skills they have. It is quite easy in this country; the UK because there is free education and even free computer training. There are also a lot of things that one could do that are government funded. Such systems are not available back in Nigeria.

You can also go for various short courses such as; childcare, social care, child minding etc. There are lots of things you can do so you can help yourself. These are the things that the Tender Care Health Initiative does.

DOMESTIC VIOLENCE (DV) INVOLVEMENT

Being a midwife was the most rewarding thing that I had ever done. I believe if I came into this world again, I would still like to be a midwife. This was because of the closeness it brought with women especially the vulnerable ones. There is nothing like vulnerability written in front of their foreheads per se. You will probably never know what any woman is going through. They come to the antenatal clinic smartly dressed in their maternity gown, wearing the correct flat shoes and even makeup and smiling. It is only when you sit down with them to ask; how are you? How do you feel today? What have you done this week? Are you sleeping okay? Are you eating well? Are you getting support? That is when the tap opens.

I could not believe the things I heard. A lot of the women had always thought that physical abuse was the only form of domestic violence. They never realised that if they had to beg for money from their spouse every time that it is financial abuse. It is incredible what some of the women go through. Some of them even work and earn, but their husbands still take their pay cheques from them, give them a weekly or monthly stipend depending on how she gets paid.

My head grew heavy in disbelief. Some of them were called idiots and stupid, and gradually they begin to believe these things, that is emotional and psychological abuse. These are all the things I came across from my years as a midwife, and I got deeply involved in supporting women experiencing domestic violence.

I took up the role of a domestic violence coordinator in the Maternity Unit at North Middlesex University Hospital, just listening, talking and advising the women. They always had a feeling of anxiety and consciousness for their safety, yet they were unable to take that first initiative of asking for help. The safety of the unborn child was discussed and considered by the safeguarding and child protection team. The welfare of the children is paramount and should be protected.

When I became a Local Authority Councillor, it was obvious and natural for me to join the safeguarding team that dealt with domestic violence. They held meetings at 2 pm on Thursdays, once a month and I always attended. Since I worked as a community midwife, I was able to work around the time. I did not take a lunch break so I would be able to use that instead of my lunch break. I always had a way of fixing time, and I am great when it comes to time management. So, this was how I got involved. The stories were just too much. It is harrowing what a pregnant woman had to go through. It was bad enough being pregnant. I have been pregnant, so I know how it feels. There is so much that can be happening to a woman's body due to hormonal changes. She is already tearful, tired, stressed up, uncomfortable, and then to add to that, the person who got her pregnant - husband or partner - who is supposed to be making her workload light is abusing her, was just not acceptable.

There was a case I will always remember. There was this young lady who attended my clinic mainly on weekends, normally on Saturdays. She was from the Asian community and had just turned eighteen or so. She came with her husband to the clinic. I had seen them several times, and she would always go home looking all happy and bubbly. As the saying goes, "Every day for the thief and one day for the owner of the house." One day she came to the clinic and amazingly her husband did not come with her. When she came, we greeted and so forth. I asked, "How are you? Are you alone today?" She said, yes that her husband was at work and could not get time off. However, before she could finish speaking tears were running down her eyes.

So, I asked her, what the matter was, if she was okay? By now she was shaking and was nervous. Either nervous from recollection of what had been happening to her or maybe worried about whether she should tell me or not. It could have also been that she was scared of going back home. These were things that came to my mind after she told me what had been happening to her. Gradually she told me. She said, "You know every time I come here, he would always come with me. He would have beaten me up before coming. The mother-in-law would call me names. They say I'm a fool and every time he comes, he's all smiling and so forth. Midwife, no it's not okay. I'm in an awful situation. I'm scared, and I don't want to go back home."

This was on a Saturday, and it was her first baby. I said okay and I called my manager on-call. I told her I had a situation here. They said okay since she had not been forced to say anything, we could attend to her. So, we called the social services out-of-hours. She said she was not going home and she did not want them to call her husband either. She did not want them to know where she was. Then she started showing us marks and scars on her body.

If it were now, the husband would have been jailed for grievous bodily harm. Sadly, in those days, domestic violence was not taken that serious until women started dying so much. Nevertheless, we sent her to a refuge, and they took over from there. She never went back. She was married and brought over here to London. Fortunately for her, she could speak a bit of English. The whole family severely maltreated her. She said she knows that when she gets home, she would still have to cook. I said, "Cooking? You're almost due to have the baby." She said, "Oh, they'll kill me." I think it was an unfortunate experience.

I think with all these experiences; I continue to highlight what women go through and why it is necessary that girls are appreciated and educated.

My mission in life is not merely to survive, but to thrive; and to do so with some passion, some compassion, some humour, and some style.

- **Maya Angelou**

Chapter Ten

CHARITY AFTER MIDWIFERY CAREER

My charity had always been something on my mind. I kept asking myself, "when I finish my midwifery what would I do? Would I turn my back on these women and the babies?" I delivered hundreds of babies in my over thirty-year career as a midwife. I found it difficult to turn my back even though I studied Law. I studied Law so I could change careers. After studying Law for about four or five years, I still did not give up midwifery. So, I could not turn my back now.

I said to myself, those vulnerable women that you care about, why not form an organisation where you can work with and support them. Tell them you are a listening ear who they can call or come to. Gradually I thought about the name. Then I remembered a name that came up when I was Mayor. A friend of mine who was a member of the Mayor's committee mentioned tender care, and I thought, oh that is nice. Because everybody kept asking, "Oh Kate, what do you want to do when you finish your term as Mayor?" I said I really wanted to remain in health, but I also wanted to work with women. And because it has to do with health, I called it Tender Care Health Initiative.

TENDER CARE HEALTH INITIATIVE

Tender Care Health Initiative was registered in 2013 as a charity for community interest company while I was still a Mayor. So, it was ready when I finished as Mayor. When I attended functions for my Mayoral role, I did a lot of speeches. For some reason, people seemed to like what I had to say, and they would always come to me, asking to see me again because they wanted to talk to me. I stayed in touch with a lot of women that I met during my time as Mayor.

Tender Care works with young, vulnerable mothers of any age with babies under the age of one. I have been working regularly with them for the past four years on Wednesdays and Thursdays. We stimulate the babies by singing baby rhymes and teaching the mothers the baby rhymes as well. We show them activities they can be doing to interact with their babies; getting them to network with other mums, to talk about their babies and baby do's and don'ts and also advising them on feeding their babies. Some of them are breastfeeding, and they want to talk to me about that. Some are bottle feeding, and they want to know if it would affect their babies because they did not breastfeed etc.

When they ask questions that require the Health Visitor, I always refer them to the Health Visitor's clinic. Sometimes they just need reassurance and are not sure if they should go to see their General Practitioner (GP). I encourage them to go and see their GP, for second opinion and peace of mind. I think they just want somebody to talk to. It is during these meetings that I came across more women with domestic violence issues. Another case quite recent, just before Christmas, was one where a mother was thrown out by the husband with her eleven-month-old baby. He happily told her that he did not need her anymore and that he was going away on holiday with his girlfriend.

I think it is terrible, vicious and crazy to tell someone you have been married to for over six years, who has your child, to go and look for a place because you are going away with your girlfriend and you would like to lock up your house. That is why I think I can never give up my work with women. She had no money, and this was financial abuse. She had been reduced to nothing which is psychological and emotional abuse as well.

One other service that Tender Care Initiative provides is to signpost cases to relevant organisations like Solace Charity that deals with domestic violence and many other issues that might arise. We also help to speak to the council to get temporary accommodation, but on this occasion, the Council could not help, which was very sad.

SICKLE CELL WORK IN THE COMMUNITY

I got involved with Sickle Cell because I came from a family where there was sickle cell running on my mother's side. When I came to England, I did not know anything about sickle cell. I remember vividly when I was expecting my first child, I had a blood test and no one explained anything to me what it was for.. They only gave me a small card that I must carry with me. Much later, when I was doing my midwifery that was when I came across the sickle cell. That was when I took a closer look at the card. It had, "Sickle trait." I said, "oh, so I have sickle trait!" Then I started reading about it. That was when I came across the various genotypes; AA, AS and SS. And I thought "oh!" I remember they did ask me to ask my husband to come and they did the blood test on him as well and they said he didn't have the trait. That was the end of the story, and nobody explained anything to me as you would expect today. So, I thought I needed to know more about this. Then I found out that the trait that I had was from my mum. My mum had a brother who was AS, and he got married to a woman who was AS as well.

I became even more interested in the sickle cell when my mum's nephew passed on from full-blown sickle cell disease. He was SS because both of his parents were AS. He was an undergraduate when he died. Then I started reading about it. Within the midwifery profession, I began meeting women with sickle cell trait which was not a problem as long as their husband did not have a trait. The most important thing is trying to explain to people and make them understand that if they have the sickle cell trait, there is no need to worry. Being an AS is not a disease it is just having an abnormal cell shape. If your husband or partner is AA, then you are okay. If you eat right and your haemoglobin (HB0) does not get so low, then you do not get pain or anything. If your husband has the sickle cell trait (AS) and also you have the sickle trait (AS), then it is more likely that one out of your four children will have the sickle cell disease (SS).That was why my mum's nephew ended up with SS, because both parents were AS. Now there are a lot of campaigns and awareness events, talking to people especially the young ones to know their genotype. The Catholic Faith encourages the young people, before getting into marriage to check their genotype; in fact, it is one of the requirements before the priest will join them together in marriage.

When I became the Mayor of Enfield, I thought to myself that some of the funds that I was going to raise would be going towards helping people with sickle cell anaemia. North Middlesex hospital where I worked did not have a proper sickle cell unit, but they had sickle cell clinics for people with sickle cell or any blood disease such as Thalassemia, suffered by people mainly from the Mediterranean.

Like I said, when you are Mayor, one of the things you have to do is choose a charity and raise funds for that charity. You can select as many charities as you like, but I picked four. The four charities were: Sickle Cell Unit at North Middlesex hospital, the second was The Voice which is a small organisation in Enfield. It is a group of women gathered together helping children with disability. Some of these women have disabled children as well. The third was a young people's organisation called Project E18. These young people had been in Care, and by the time they leave Care at the age of eighteen, they are deemed old enough to look after themselves. Some of them are just sent away into the community with no guidance or mentor. These are the ones who probably end up in very rough hands. They end up in criminal paths. It's quite easy for them to fall into the hands of hardened criminals like drug pushers who might use them to perform their illicit activities.

I heard about the project which was the brainchild of Jermaine Defoe, a well-known footballer formerly of Tottenham Hotspur, who now plays for Rangers in the Scottish league. He is the founder of Project E18. I thought it was a good charity and I would like to raise funds for them. Project E18 mentors young people who have been in the care system. What they do is help get them back into the system, to re-integrate them into the community without them getting into trouble. The money I raised for them was to train mentors who were going to mentor the young people. The fourth was another sickle cell support group charity in Enfield.

I raised £44,000 in one year. The highest any Mayor had ever raised, and no one has managed to beat that record as of the time of writing. I gave North Middlesex Hospital £15,000. I gave The Voice £5,000, Enfield Sickle Cell Support team £5,000, £1,000 to the Stroke Action in Enfield and the balance of £18,000 to Project 18.

To raise the funds required a lot of planning. I was swamped most of the time. First of all, I had a team that I called the Mayor's Committee. There were twelve people in this committee, and we had meetings in my house to plan the events we were going to host. First of all, mayors do have what we call "Civic Service." As a Catholic, I had my Civic Mass at my local church, St Edmunds Roman Catholic Church. I remember very well; it was on the 22nd of July 2012, the air was dry, the sky was clear and beautiful. It was just a fantastic day. Before the Civic Mass, my committee had a series of meetings at my house. We were thinking of what we should do on that day; should we go to church and then we all go home or make it a day of fun, networking and entertainment? Then we said no we needed to make some money.

So, we made a brochure. You know Nigerians are very good at brochures. We asked people to come and advertise in the brochure, and they did. I think we charged £100 for a full page and £50 for half a page. My daughter the Mayoress who is an IT professional and web designer with good artistic skills organised all the advertisements before sending them to the printers. We saved a lot of money on the design by her doing all that, so all we paid for was to print the brochures. The brochures were sold at £1 each on the day of the Civic Mass. We raised a lot of money from that. It was a perfect way of raising funds. Brochures are done in every Nigerian function these days especially within the churches as well. On that very day, we had buckets as well asking people to donate. We also gave out envelopes asking them to donate. We explained to them what we were raising funds for.

We had a sickle cell dinner and dance at Tottenham Selby Centre. The reason for using this venue was because Enfield did not have a big enough hall. The hall they had was too expensive, but the Selby Centre hall was reasonable. A lot of people came out to help. The hall was paid for by Mr Amaechi Ani who is the Founder and Proprietor of IQ Express. This meant that I did not have to pay for it from the money we raised on the day.

Also, on that very day, I had big donations too. People who donated over a thousand pounds were: Mr Charles Sylvester Enukowhate of Express Securities and Mrs Oby Ezeilo. Their contributions formed the bulk of the money we used to pay for the expenses we incurred. We had other donations especially from those who advertised on the brochure as well. We sold tickets at £25 each. Any other bulk expenses that we had were already taken care of by the people we invited.

We also had a fun run in September of that year. People paid to participate. We made T-shirts, and Barclays Bank Nigeria donated £1,000. We also had raffle tickets.

Wilko in Edmonton Green invited me to open their shop at 8 am, and they were giving my charity £500. I said, yeah! Even if they wanted me at 6 am, I would be there. Another shop that wanted me to open their shop also brought a cheque of £500 in support of the mayor's charity.

Some people on their own just continued raising funds doing various things for the mayor's charity because they were quite good at it. They just came back with money for the charity. It is incredible what people can do and give for a good cause, their time and money, it was awesome.

FAWP- FORUM FOR AFRICAN, AFRICAN CARIBBEAN AND ASIAN WOMEN IN POLITICS.

I cannot tell exactly how I got into politics, but I can explain a bit how it happened. While I was working as a community midwife, I met a lot of women with issues; on housing, environment, social services etc. You were not just delivering babies; you were an advocate and mouthpiece for these women because they tell you things. For example, when a woman with a newborn baby gets a home visit from me, she might say her neighbours are making so much noise or complain of other issues. I will be the one left with the burden to find a solution.

What I did usually was phone the Council and tell them that this woman has got such and such issues, whom shall I contact? At a point, I said to myself, "ah ah, all these things I'm asking them, who are all these people they are getting the answers from?" I soon found out that they are called Councillors. I asked myself, "how did they get there?" I made other enquiries, and someone asked me, "Are you in a Party?" I said no, he said, "You have to be in a political Party." He continued by saying, "But Kate, you can talk. You could easily be a Councillor."

Gradually I found myself looking for the political parties to join. First of all, I thought I liked The Conservative because they had money; they could easily do this and that. Unfortunately, I did not know the difference between both parties. When I finally made up my mind to join a political party, I sat down to read about policies, election manifestoes of the Conservative and Labour Parties and by the time I finished reading I made my discovery, I said, "No! No!! No!!! I'm 100% pure Labour. I'm not Conservative in any way at all. NO WAY!!!"

I am from an ethnic minority, I am a woman, I am an ordinary worker etc., how can I be Conservative? The values of the Labour party made me join them. They cared about the workers, about women, and about the ethnic minority. These were all issues that I also cared about. That was how and why I joined the Labour Party.

Within the Labour Party, I attended a lot of meetings. So, now every evening that I was free I was attending a meeting; either the Labour Party meeting or women's meeting. By now I had also joined Enfield Women's Aid. Apart from the hospital, Enfield Women's Aid was the other charity. Then came the Council Domestic Violence Coordinator Support Group. Because of all these meetings, my friends used to say to me, "Kate anytime I call you're never around, always in meetings. What kind of meetings are these?" They would ask "How much do they pay you?" I would tell them that I was not getting paid and this surprised my friends.

I told my friends that I go there to listen. And while I was listening, I was learning. They would say, "Keep going. me, I want something with money." I would tell them, okay, that I would carry on. That was what I kept doing and gradually I found myself becoming more active, so I went on to become the Women Ethnic Minority Officer in the Party. I met some of our people whom I told about joining a political Party, and they used to say, "Oh, no I don't want." This "Oh, no, I don't want" attitude has affected us, even till today. It is the reason why we do not have much of our Nigerians or Africans in the local government; they are only attracted by the money. If we had considered politics since the early sixties when Africans and African Caribbeans arrived in the UK, we should have had more MPs, Ministers, Councillors and Leaders of Council from the Black and Minority Ethnic (BAME) by now.

I supported and helped some of our women or those whom I managed to convince to get them in my Borough here in Enfield. As of the time I became a councillor, there was no Nigerian Councillor in the Borough. But as of the time I had my break in 2014, we already had four Nigerians; three women and one man. I got them there. I worked hard to convince them to come to meetings. I told them that if they get involved, it might lead to something bigger. Nothing you learn in life is useless. Any act that we learn is always useful, one way or the other.

I discussed and advised which meetings to attend, becoming a school governor, attending Labour Party meetings, and being an active participant. If asked to take a role, take it, and you can learn on the job. I remember during the Local Government candidate nomination, they said they did not want to nominate or be nominated to be Councillors yet. I told them, "go on you must put your name down." I remember staying up until 3 am on the phone completing the form with one of the women because I wanted her to submit the form before midday the next day. Another lady said no because she was not ready. I said if you do not do it now, it is going to be in another four years, so get on with it and submit.

One of them submitted her form just ten minutes before the closing time. I made sure I gave kind words about them because people in the council did not know them. I wrote that they were my sisters, they were good and hardworking, and that was how they got selected. The climax and happiness for me was that both ladies from Nigeria were successful in that year's local election and were elected as Councillors.

As for me, the focus was making sure that I not only worked hard on the Council but I also portrayed Nigeria as a positive country with positive people. I crowned it all on the day I was inaugurated as the Mayor of Enfield. I wore the full Nigerian attire with the *gele* (Nigerian headgear). It had never happened. That was my pride. I am a proud Nigerian, and I am proud of where I come from. I am proud of what I have achieved, not just for myself but for other women.

I climbed a ladder. I did not kick the ladder away. I held the ladder for other women and men to come up and join me. I am happy that they came. I feel good and happy about that. I have no regrets as to whether or not I fulfilled my duties while I was at the Council.

When I was Mayor, I made sure I did the job well so that the opportunity remained open for other Nigerians who aspire to get there. That is what is called empowerment. That is what is called inspiration, and that is what is called holding the door without being selfish. I do not expect any of them to remember me because that was not the point. That was not why I did it. I did it for myself because I wanted to feel complete. For me to think that I have done a job properly, it is by passing on my knowledge. This is what I call transferred knowledge. You transfer your experience and your skill to someone else. By so doing, you know you have done your best, and that is what I believe in. This should be happening more often.

But unfortunately, it is not happening because most women for some reason or the other seem not to be happy within ourselves for other women. They want to run other women down. When you see what is happening amongst women you will begin to think; who do you trust? Who do you continue to work with? Who do you really know? I have come across a lot of women. I have come across those, whom I thought I knew, but their attitude, their behaviour, their selfishness, and their greed made me realise nobody could ever say they know someone fully well. You may know someone peripherally, but inwards, no. Most women are as changeable as the chameleon.

My long-term goal for FAWP is to continue to engage with more women from black and minority ethnic backgrounds for political awareness and leadership through seminars and conferences. I am most grateful to our two Patrons; Member of Parliament, Honourable Seema Malhotra for Feltham & Heston and Honourable Kate Osamor for Edmonton, for their commitment to FAWP. The MPs were available at conferences and seminars to educate, inspire and to answer questions. Some women say they do not know you had to join a political party to become a councillor. These are the kind of things we want people to know. If you want to know more about politics and how it works, then it would be a good idea to join a political party. Not everyone in a political party even wants to be a politician. Some say they just wanted to understand what politics is about because they have seen some politicians arguing and sometimes shouting in the House of Commons and they want to know the reason for all the commotion because, at times, the scenario looks like men and women behaving badly.

CATCH THEM YOUNG

The idea for Catch Them Young which is a part of the FAWP came about when I was in the university studying Law and had to work with a lot of young people. While I was studying and revising with them, I decided that they should call me Aunty Kate instead of Kate. This was to remind them we were not mates even though we happened to be in the school at the same time. From working with them, I found out that the majority of young people want certain things, but they leave it for later. It would be nice to meet them when they are even younger because by the time they get to the university or even secondary school age they would have formed an idea of what they want to do.

From my many talks in secondary schools, I discovered that the majority of our young people do not understand politics or even the way their school is run. They do not know who runs the country. They hear the name Tony Blair, David Cameron or Theresa May, but who are they? How did they get there? These are the things the majority of women and young people do not know or understand; hence they may not have the facts. I believe if we are going to be talking to young people about politics and trying to engage them, then it is necessary to start by explaining politics and how it affects our daily activities in our homes, schools, churches, housing, environment, health etc. Why do we have to wait until they are mamas and papas before we start talking to them about it? Let us catch them young while they are still in primary or secondary school. Out of twenty, there would be one who would be interested in politics in the future.

We could start by asking them about their school; who decides the policies and guidelines for running the schools? How are the schools funded? What is Politics? Who do you think a politician is? Can you name some? Who is he or she? This is just a fun way of introducing politics to young people.

We launched Catch Them Young on the 22nd of October, 2016. The reason we launched it was to start talking to our young people about politics and leadership from an early age. That would help them get interested in politics and probably groom them to be leaders. The organisation is not just open to ethnic minorities; it is for everyone from any ethnicity or background because when I go to schools, I speak to all of them.

ENFIELD WOMEN'S AID

My work with Enfield Women's Aid started when I was working at North Middlesex Hospital as a midwife and the domestic violence coordinator in the hospital. I knew that if we were helping in the hospital, there must be an organisation in the community also assisting women. When I made enquiries, I found that the organisation is called Enfield Women's Aid, so I joined them. They also had Refuges where they refer women to. I was pleased that I joined them because that helped to expand my knowledge with regards to what happens to the women and their children when they want to take refuge and leave their home. I did not know about refuges until I joined the Enfield Women's Aid.

I joined them as an ordinary member, and I also did visits and raised funds for the organisation. Members of the organisation are allowed to visit the refuges to see how the new intakes were settling.

When I was Mayor, I visited the refuges and Local Authority Care homes as well.

ACTIVITIES IN CHURCH

Both of my parents were staunch Catholics, and in those days, you had to follow in the footsteps of your parents, and that included practising the same faith. When I came over to England, I carried on with the same. When I lost my husband, without thinking about it, I noticed that for calmness, stronger faith and strength, one tends to lean more towards the church. We went to church as regularly as before, but I became more active in the church and helped out when necessary.

We had a small organisation called Cornerstone, which was set up by a few people from the church and I joined them. It was just again about raising funds for the vulnerable. Gradually, Cornerstone became self-sufficient that it started running itself and we pulled out. It is now peer-led.

The Catholic Church has made it possible for the public to join the priests in giving out Holy Communion. The priest invited you. You do not go to the priest and say I want to be part of that group. I think the priest keeps an eye out for people and select people they want to join and invite them to become Eucharistic Ministers. One day, the priest called me, he said, "Kate I'd like you to be one of the Eucharistic Ministers." What you do is during Holy Communion, you join the priest to distribute Holy Communion to the people. You are either distributing the Host or the Wine. I said yes, I would gladly. "You'll get your training," he added. Also, as Eucharistic Minister, you can go out to the community to give communion to the sick and the house-bound, and I did that as well. You also have to learn the special prayer you say when you get to the house. As Eucharistic Ministers, we went on retreats. I asked myself, "who am I to be holding the Host," and I feel blessed by the privilege.

I was one of the founding members of St Edmund's Nigerian Catholic Community which was formed in 1998, and it is still going quite strong. Some other ethnic groups have emulated us; the Ghanaians, the Sierra-Leoneans etc. but we were the first. We did a lot of work and fundraising to support the church; during bazaars or fete we cooked Nigerian food and sold to the people who attended. So, instead of hot dogs and whatever, people got proper Nigerian food. All the money we made, we donated to the church. Individuals from the group state what they were comfortable to cook and bring. I may decide to make *jallof* rice. I might buy £5 rice, cook it and make up to £50 and all money raised goes to the church. Someone else may bring *moi moi* (bean dumpling) and another person, fried rice or say I would make Nigerian salad, which is made with baked beans, boiled eggs and so many other things all mixed up and it's very nice. Someone else might bring chicken, coleslaw, *akara* (bean cake), etc.

Inasmuch as we made Nigerian food, we were inclusive and catered for everybody, and people were always ready to try any of our Nigerian dishes. I liked cooking, but at these events I always made coleslaw. With my special knife, I hand shred the cabbage, grate the carrots, add small white onions and mix all with low-calorie mayonnaise. It always looked inviting and appealing. My friends called it Kate's speciality. It all sounds easy, but I can tell you that the shredding of cabbage could take up to four hours depending on the quantity needed. We did this about twice a year- the bazaar and fete, and we usually raised about £300 or more for the church. This was one of our activities in St Edmund's, and there were many other ways we supported the church.

Even when I am in Nigeria for Christmas, on the day, while everybody is busy preparing rice, cow or goat meat, I would be busy from about five in the morning, washing, and washing loads of cabbage, carrots, cucumber and onions for coleslaw. I am very particular about washing and doing everything myself. For the fact it is called my speciality, I don't want any 'unnecessary stories' with it. Once it is ready, I share it out to as many people in the village as I want. My dad and mum always look forward to it. May they rest in peace.

We also have the Igbo Catholic Community, which is under the umbrella of Nigerian Chaplaincy England and Wales. Within the Igbo Catholic Community, we have

Christian mothers *Ndinne* and an individual is called *Ezinne*. When I joined the Christian Mother's group, meetings and Mass were held at St. Mellitus Catholic Church at Finsbury Park every first Saturday and second Sunday of the month. Now, we have moved to St Edmund's Roman Catholic Church in Edmonton, which is good for me because it is in my locality. On Sundays, we have refreshments and networking after Mass in the hall. I joined this group by my late mother's advice and encouragement, but unfortunately, I had an awful experience at some point. In a group of Christian mothers, I least expect the attitude and behaviour of some mothers. I reached the point of writing a letter of resignation, as I felt I had better things to do than that. You see, I normally would take my youngest daughter with me, as I want to give her the opportunity of seeing the other part of church activities and the contribution of the mothers, regrettably, she saw something different.

I am the Coordinator of the group at present, and I have held that post for some years now. Hopefully, we will have elections soon so I can be relieved of duty. For reasons, best known to me, I will refrain from expressing my experience of the last couple of years. In the Igbo Catholic Community, we have a general coordinator who is Sir Longinus Ezinna Iwu. We also take part in other activities like Igbo Day which is held once a year. On this day we celebrate Igbo culture with a display of our cultural dance, more traditional foods with other Igbo communities in the UK and friends of the Igbos. It is very motivating.

On our Igbo Mass day, after Mass we go to the hall to celebrate together and network. Sometimes, families may want to come and do thanksgiving celebration, so there is the opportunity for them as well to do that at the Igbo Mass.

Ndinne holds their meetings first Saturday of every month at the Scout Hall in St Edmund's Church. We also have a uniform. We wear our uniform on special occasions like in the May month of Mary our Mother.

My other church activity is with the Nigerian Catholic Chaplaincy. Here again, I am a member of the Nigerian Chaplaincy Catholic Women Organization (NCCWO). The NCCWO have meetings once every month. We take active roles in things that happen in the chaplaincy; thanksgiving, harvest and bazaar, etc. We also have our uniform as well.

Another activity is the Enfield Nigerian Community, which we formed in 2014, and is still growing. The aim is to get the Nigerian people living in Enfield together to know themselves just like other communities do and maybe then enthuse them into politics as well. Those are things we are always looking at, and it seems a bit difficult to gather them at the moment, but we will continue to persevere.

In most of the organisations I belong to, I am either the president or vice president. It is not because I am the best leader, but I believe I have a lot of the qualities required of a leader. First and foremost, a leader is a servant who has been elected to serve. Most have listening ears, communication skills, humility, sensitivity and ability to absorb direct and indirect abuse, bullying and other unfavourable challenges. The most challenging thing I experienced was allegations against me; you try to maintain calmness as you absorb all and resist the exchange of words and confrontation. Some will go out of their way to manufacture lies, just to discredit others. But there comes a time in one's life where maturity and wisdom rule you, and I am happy that I have chosen that pathway to surmount those adults who will never grow up.

I learned long ago, never to wrestle with a pig.
You get dirty, and besides, the pig likes it.

-George Bernard Shaw

Chapter Eleven

POLITICAL MEANING

When asked what politics means to me, I would say that it is about a group of people with the same ideas getting together to make decisions about running a country, and want to help others in one way or the other. Politics affects everyone in different ways, and for me, I believe there is politics in everything we do in life, and that includes the churches and mosques.

This group of people that we call politicians, care about people's health, they care about the environment, and they care about other things that affect the individual. They value people and have empathy for others. A group of people with the same ideologies appear to stick together, and they tend to belong to the same political party, depending on what their beliefs are.

I agree 100% that not everyone in politics care about people's welfare; they may be there for their personal gain. Hence, this is why we have different types of political Parties in the UK; we have the Labour Party, Conservative Party, Liberal Democrats, and the UKIP. Each of them has something to offer. Even in the Labour Party, you have someone who is just there because they want to hold a position and for their name to be heard. That kind of person might not want to help anybody at all. They are just there for their own good. Even though we generally believe that politicians are a group of people who are there to help in the running of the country, there are still one or two out of ten who might be there only for their selfish benefits.

Now how do I ensure that the people and even the young ones whom I mentored and encouraged to join politics and the Labour Party or helped become councillors have a good set of values and really care for people, and not just because I wanted them to make up the numbers? This is very difficult, to say the least. It is almost like parents; you have your children, you teach them the good values of life, you show them the do's and don'ts, and as far as you are concerned you have done your entire job well, and you believe your child is going to be a good person and a respectable citizen. But woe betide you that your child was caught stealing something or doing some other wrongful act. So, it is just the same thing. You can help them into politics and teach them everything, but there may be someone amongst all of them who is not there for what you stand for. They are there to make up the numbers but also, they selfishly know where they want to climb to, and they know the only way they can get there is through politics.

The fact is some people do not care what they have to do to achieve their selfish goals and sadly, that is life. Even more recently, you saw it during the Brexit campaign. We have Boris Johnson and Michael Gove, both campaigning to leave Europe. Only now did we find out that both Boris Johnson and Michael Gove wanted to be Prime Minister. Either both of them did not know, or pretend not to know what either was aiming for. The only person the general public knew wanted to be Prime Minister was Johnson, but unknown to him his friend, Gove also wanted the role. The saying, "It takes a friend to soak a friend," happened in this situation. Sadly, this is what happens at times in politics. Politicians are not the most open-minded people.

They have their ways of being nice and ways of being very bad, and I have met a lot of them.

I am a politician saying all these, but I have to be honest because that is my nature. People have trust issues with politicians. Now, do people trust me? I would rather say generally, people do not trust politicians. However, I always say to people, do not judge everyone the same, judge people individually. I love politics in Britain because it is where policies are put in practice, and we serve the local communities as promised during the campaign trail. Campaign means campaign, seriously for six good weeks, and a win is a win because you merited it. On the election day my, Fitbit clocked over twenty kilometres knocking at over six thousand doors asking for votes, but no bags of rice or money was given to the voters as it happens in some countries.

I have been asked many times about politics in Nigeria. To be honest I would have loved to go back to Nigeria to practice the good skills that I have acquired, but regrettably, politics in the developing world is dirty, dangerous and never by merit. So much rigging of ballot papers and bought votes. For women, they are marginalised; you need to have a godfather to further your political career.

I want to believe that people trust me because I am a very open-minded person. I have worked long enough in the community for people to know that I am a sincere politician who is not there only for my good. I have also shown by example, by not only being there and behaving like an excellent Nigerian but also encouraging other Nigerians to excel. I think people should trust me and say to others that I am not just there for myself. I am quite happy that people trust me, especially young people who invite me to a lot of their conferences and events to speak, which says a lot because you have to trust someone before you ask them to come to speak at your conference. They also call me for advice and ask for meetings with me. I think they probably see me as a mother figure and as someone who has achieved what they would also like to accomplish in the future, or someone who is approachable and always ready to help and has a listening ear. Sometimes, they just want a role model to narrate how I achieved success while raising four children on my own. My children are all graduates, working and handling their responsibilities. It is not easy in this country with four children, on your own.

In 2014, I ran for the parliamentary seat. There were 108 applicants, and out of that number, I was amongst the last three candidates, and that made me very happy. For me, it was a success because I did not want to go for the parliamentary seat in the first place. It just happened that one day, my youngest daughter came back from work, and as usual, I was giving her a run-down of my day, then out of the blue she said to me "Mummy, why don't you apply?" I said, "No I don't want to." She pushed further by saying, "Those people applying are not better than you." I told her that I did not think I was ready. The reason why I said I was not prepared was that if you want to be an MP, there is training for prospective parliamentarians that you had to attend. I never participated in the training, so I wondered where do I start. I would not even know how to apply or answer questions let alone do other things. But you know what? She was on me and never gave up. Through her persuasion, I thought to myself, why not? Let's go for it!

So, I requested for the application forms, which was sent to me by email. I know how long it took me to answer all the questions and it was all done online. I was so happy that at the end of it, I did not just apply but I was on to the Long list of twelve, then onto the Shortlist of three. I did not win, but for me, it was a great success because in a race, you usually give the gold medal to number one, to number two silver, and number three, bronze. I am a winner even though I came third and I am glad to say my daughter made me try and I put in my best effort. Otherwise, I would not have known my capability, and that is the reason why I always tell people to believe in themselves. During the parliamentary seat run, I did not practice what I preached. If I had practised what I have always taught people, then I do not see why I should have doubted myself. I should have believed in myself because that is what I always say to people; to always believe in yourself and always say that you can.

Although it might be that I am too hard on myself, I think the doubt I had was because I had not gotten the necessary training and I did not know how the questions were framed. It was never a doubt linked with a lack of faith in myself. I believe if I had the right training, I would have been more equipped for the questions.

The campaign was very exhausting. I had lots of friends who came out to help while some saboteurs also organised themselves, calling from their homes and outside the Borough, discouraging members from voting for me. In life, no one must expect to be liked by all. It is not uncommon, but one thing we must not forget is "while you are pointing one finger at someone, the remaining four are directed at you." It is a warning because tomorrow it could be your turn. I am a comeback kid, and after four years away from the Local Government, I won my fourth term in the last local election that held on May the 3rd, 2018. I was very excited and happy with myself. However, looking back, I can say that I was not really out of the limelight in those four years. It looked like it on paper, but in reality, I was always out campaigning during General Election, London Mayoral Election, European Election, so I never really stopped. I love talking to people; my life has always been in the community, remember I was a community midwife for over thirty years, so you can see why I never stop working with people. It is my life.

A leader is best when people barely know he exists, when his work is done, his aim fulfilled, they will say: we did it ourselves.

- Lao Tzu

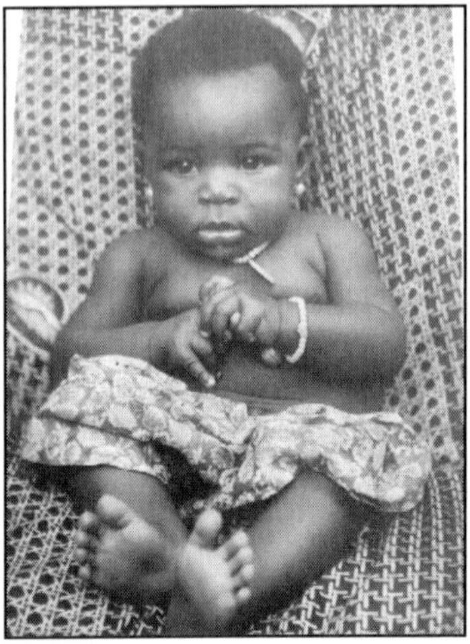

Three months old

13-14 years old

16 yrs old

17 years old

17 years old

17 years old

On first holiday in Enugu with her dearest cousin late Levi Ezeasor *(Okwuluora Nanka)*

Age 18 yrs

Age 18 with friend Irene

Age 20 with friends from Loretta Teachers Training College Adazi, Anambra

Age 20 with best friend since childhood Mercy far left

Age 21 with friends from Loretta Teachers Training College Adazi, Anambra. Kate posing with mum's clothes borrowed without her permission.

Wedding photo of Kate with her late husband Festus Ifeanyichukwu Anolue in 1971

Kate in Balham, London displaying her first two coats

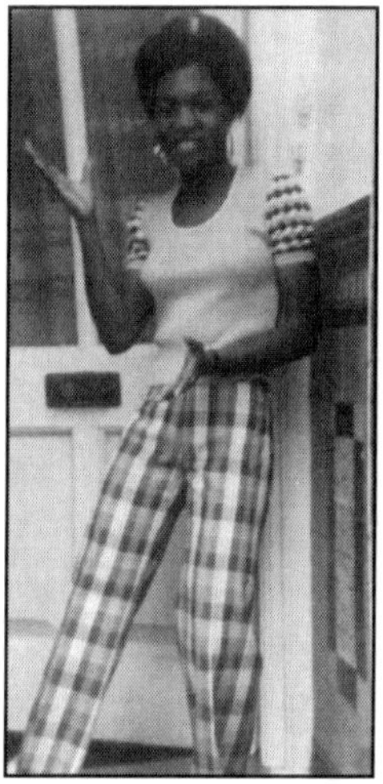

Mother of one
showing off her figure

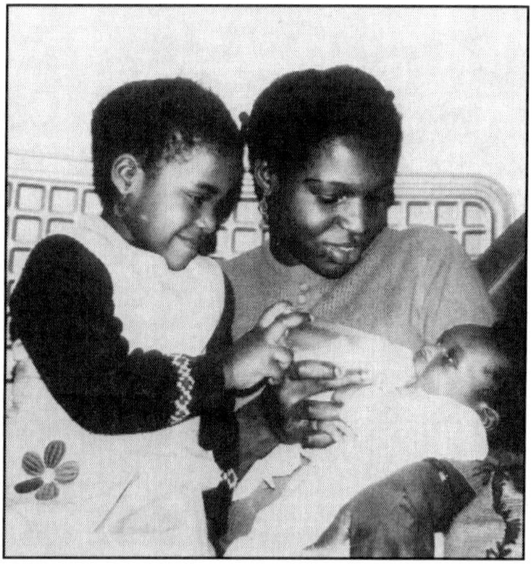

Didi helping to feed her brother Amaechi

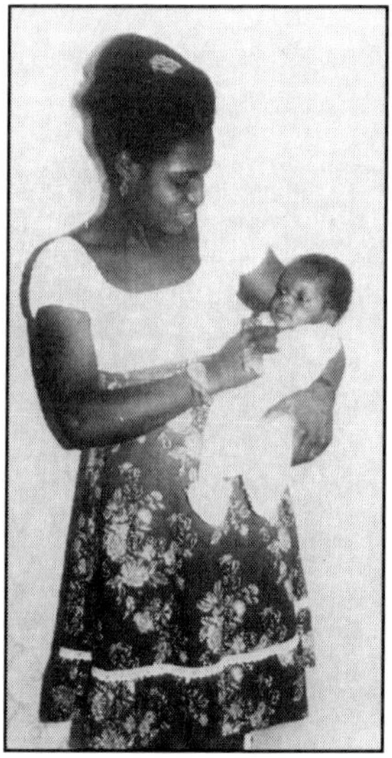

With Amaechi,
second child

Didi with Amaechi

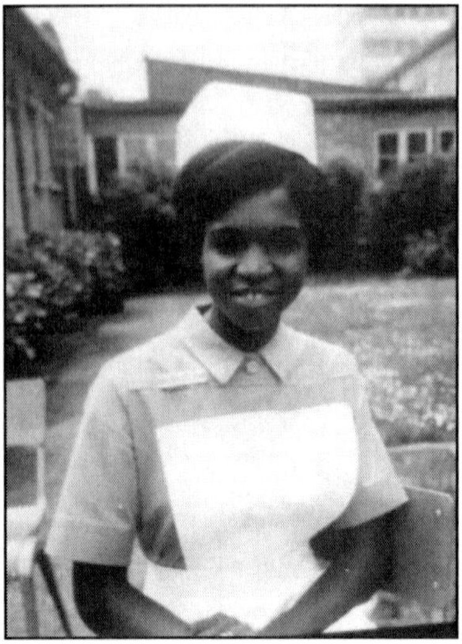

First day as student nurse at North Middlesex University Hospital in May 1972

With classmates on first day as student nurse

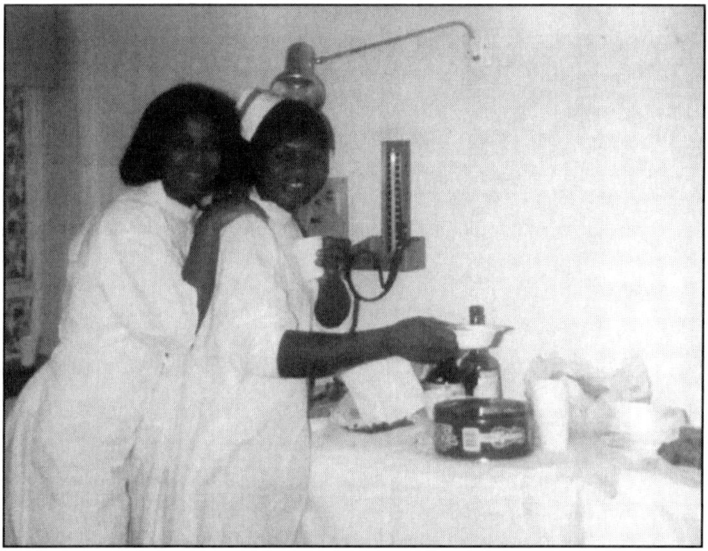

With her colleague enjoying a short
break in labour ward

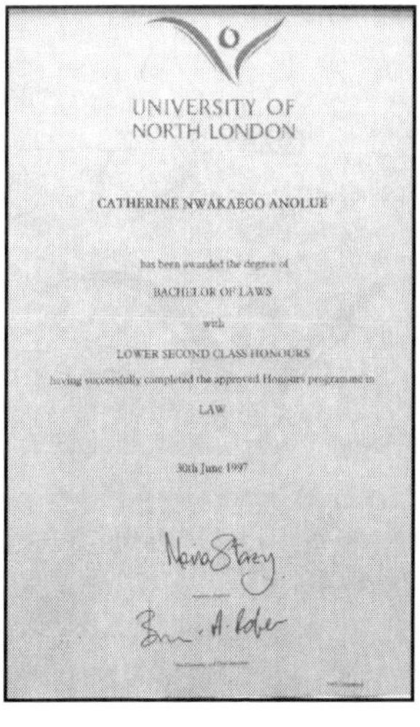

UNIVERSITY OF
NORTH LONDON

CATHERINE NWAKAEGO ANOLUE

has been awarded the degree of

BACHELOR OF LAWS

with

LOWER SECOND CLASS HONOURS

having successfully completed the approved Honours programme in

LAW

30th June 1997

Kate newly elected Councillor
in 2002, with Cllrs. Andreas
Constantinides and Betty Costello

Kate as a community midwifery sister in 1985

With best friend Mercellina (Mercy / Lina) In 1989

Visit to Didi at Southampton University

Kate receives Honorary Freeman of The Borough of Enfield Award, 2007. From left her friend Mrs Cecilia Eke, Janine Anolue – daughter-in-law, Children: Chukwuma, Chinelo, Amaechi and Councillor Nneka Keazor

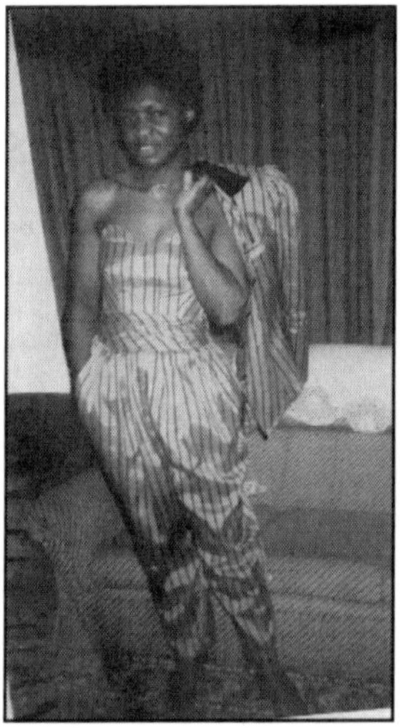

Kate celebrates her 40th birthday

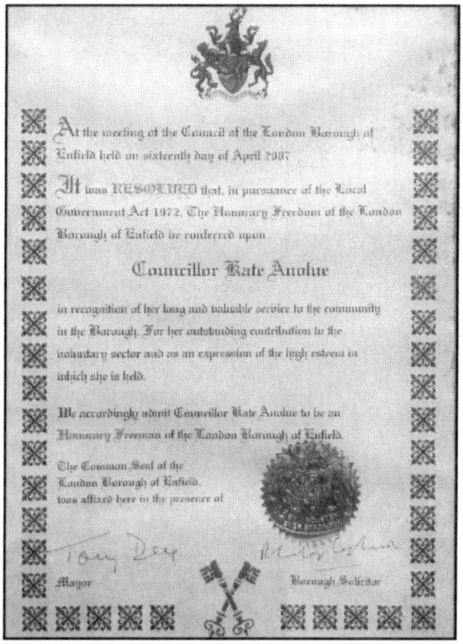

At the meeting of the Council of the London Borough of Enfield held on sixteenth day of April 2007

It was RESOLVED that, in pursuance of the Local Government Act 1972, The Honorary Freedom of the London Borough of Enfield be conferred upon

Councillor Kate Anolue

in recognition of her long and valuable service to the community in the Borough. For her outstanding contribution to the voluntary sector and as an expression of the high esteem in which she is held.

We accordingly admit Councillor Kate Anolue to be an Honorary Freeman of the London Borough of Enfield.

The Common Seal of the London Borough of Enfield, was affixed here in the presence of

Tony Dey

Mayor

Borough Solicitor

Kate and other recipients of Honorary Freeman of The Borough of Enfield Award 2007, conferred by The Worshipful Mayor, Councillor Dey

With colleague at a Labour Party Conference

With the then Prime Minister's Wife, Cherie Blair

With Councillor Christiana During of Upper Edmonton and Cherie Blair

A visit to 10 Downing Street with star singer Patti Boulaye, Dr Eugene Mgbemena and other guests at the launch of African in Diaspora conference

Kate with parents and siblings, December 1983

Kate with parents and siblings, December 1993

With parents and siblings at parents 50th -
Golden wedding anniversary

Last family photo before Kate left for England,1970. Arrow pointing Kate's one and only special sister

With children on holiday at Disney World Paris

Photo of Kate's mum – Princess Veronica Egbeichi Ezeasor *(Okwesilieze Umuagbala)* December 1983

A visit to Nigeria with children in 1993

Kate with parents and siblings, December 1993

Kate's parents, Chief Fidelis Ezeobuoha Ezeasor *(Okwuolisa)* and Princess Veronica Egbeichi Ezeasor *(Okwesilieze Umuagbala)*

Kate with late Sir Prince S N C Ezeugwa, KSC *(Onowu Nanka)*

Kate on cruise in Hawaii, 2008

On holiday in Canada with her brother Amaechi Ezeasor and daughter Chinelo

At a community event

Installation of Chieftaincy Title of *Adajelumba Tulugo* 1 of Nanka on December 24th 2008

HRH Igwe G N Ofomata (*Obu Nanka of Nanka*) confers Kate with the Chieftaincy title

Kate happy with her new Chieftaincy title

The new Chief with her entourage walking round and greeting people

Sitting with mum and son Amaechi

Kate with children Amaechi & Chinelo and her brother *Ichie* Arinze Ezeasor *(Nwachinemelu)*

Traditional dancers entertaining during the celebration

The new Chief and her mum and
Princess Veronica Egbeichi Ezeasor
(Okwesilieze Umuagbala)

With children Amaechi & Chinelo and
best friend Lina and her daughter

With brother Ichie Arinze Ezeasor *(Nwachinemelu)*

With fourth brother Chukwudi Ezeasor (pet name *Udinwa)*

With her two nieces

With her sister-in-law Odinaka

With siblings and relatives

With best friend Lina

With cousin Prof. Dr Dan Ezeasor

First installation ceremony as Mayor of Enfield 2012

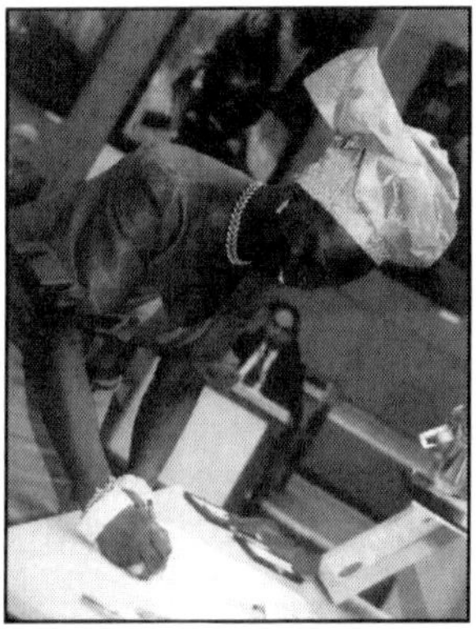

Kate signing the Register of Acceptance as Mayor of Enfield

Kate leaving the Council Chambers to be robed

With daughter Chinelo Anyanwu The Mayoress

With dear friend Jenny Chika Okafor

With Deputy Mayor & wife and Kate's supporters from Nanka

From far left Late Chief Kyrian Eke, Professor Irukwu, Mayoress Chinelo Anyanwu, Justice Anthony Iguh, Mayor Kate and Lolo Monica Ekeocha.

Kate giving her acceptance speech

With daughter Chinelo Anyanwu The Mayoress

Acknowledging and thanking her colleagues & supporters

Council Chambers

With outgoing Mayor center, Councillor Christiana During.

With Eucharia Ibekwe, Christiana Adamu and Rita Melifonwu.

With some Igwe Cabinet Members in Nanka

With two brother; Chief Barrister Chiedozie Ezeasor *(Ikeoha Nanka)* and Ichie Arinze Ezeasor *(Nwachinemelu)*

With friends Rita Melifonwu and Christiana Adamu.

With Justice Cecilia Uzoewulu and her grandchildren DeeDee and Kosa Keazor

With best friend Lina

With a friend at an award ceremony

With colleagues in front of Taj Mahal, India for Women Empowerment Conference

Adajelumba Tulugo 1 of Nanka fan

With HRH Igwe Godwin O Ezeilo (*Obu* Nanka of Nanka) and wife Ocheze.

With granddaughter Kamsi

Granddaughter Kamsi posing

At a party with Christiana Adamu

At a party with brother Chief Barrister Chiedozie and Lotanna Chima (*Enyi* Nnewi)

Kate posing at best friend Lina's son's wedding 2018, Dallas

With Chief Nnia Nwodo President General Ohanaeze Ndi Igbo

At a party with friends; Christiana Adamu, Rufina Onyechere and Chioma Obi-Nwagwu

With Nkechi Okezuronye at IFAC festival 2018

9th June 2018

At inauguration of Adaure Igbo Women Association, UK & Ireland where Kate is Vice President 1

With Chioma Obi-Nwagwu and Margaret Chukwudi

Kate posing at Adaure inauguration

With Councillor Nneka Keazor at Christiana Adamu's daughter wedding, 2018

With Aqueen Ibeto (Vice President Ohanaeze) at installation of Ohanaeze Ndi Igbo Officers and Kate as Women Leader Ohanaeze

Kate receiving award at an award ceremony, 2017

Kate giving victory speech at
local election 2018

With Hon. Kate Osamor
MP for Edmonton

With Hon. Joan Ryan MP for
Enfield North at local election
May 2018

With Barrister Jacqueline
Mazelli afternoon,
summer 2018

Kate with children on her 70th birthday, 2019

Chapter Twelve

FASHION, FUN & RELATIONSHIP

When I look back at my life, I do not think I had any vice. If I had to choose one, however, it would be my clothes. For me, it may be a good or bad habit. I do not drink alcohol or smoke. I am just a happy person. I think my best way of expressing happiness is by dressing up. I like to dress up, and I usually get caught up when I go shopping. If I find something that I like, I have to buy it. If I do not buy it, I would always think how nice that outfit would have looked on me. I like dressing up; hence, I am very conscious of what I eat. This is because if you dress up to look nice, you have to have the figure for the outfit too. Clothes fitting on your body is an integral part of looking nice.

This did not just start when I came to England. It began from back home in Nigeria. There is something I did back home with regards to fashion that I can scarcely believe even now. I have not shared this story before with anyone because I was very embarrassed. You see, when I got engaged to my late husband, he always sent me clothes from England. I can vividly remember a gorgeous, soft, and silky short skirt. It had lovely flowers at the trim, and I loved to wear this skirt very often, with a nice top, and obviously show off. I was good at that. While wearing it, my head would swell, not necessarily with pride but because I was conscious that everybody was looking at me, and I enjoyed soaking in all the attention. I did it with a swagger.

In fact, I had a pet name that they used to call me. My pet name was Katyisque. When anyone called me Katyisque, my goodness! My head would swell even more, and I swaggered harder. I tell you something, when I came to England; I could not believe that the gorgeous, soft, and silky short skirt that I liked to show off with was actually a slip. I could not believe that all those years, I was wearing a slip like a skirt and showing off! I can laugh about it now, but it was not funny when I found out. As far as everybody else was concerned, they knew that Kate gets all these fantastic things from England, so everybody believed it was a skirt. I only found out because I went shopping and I saw more of it on the lingerie section with the bras and knickers. I could not tell anybody the fashion atrocity I committed in Nigeria. I believe that kind of ignorance was inexcusable; this is the first time I am telling this story. I have never even told my children. I am sure if I had any photo of me wearing it, it would make for really good viewing. Now that you know, please feel free not to share this ignorant, embarrassing phase of a former Mayor's life with anyone. Thank you very much.

It was very short, but I was not bothered because my fiancé bought it for me, so who the hell could say anything about it. He was not there, but he liked me dressing up, so I would dress up, take photos, and send it to him. Also, probably being a man, my fiancé may just be filled with joy admiring my nice figure, not realising that I was wearing the 'slip' he sent me as a skirt. Phew!! This is how far back my fashion went, and I am glad I have not committed any such fashion atrocities since then.

You know I was just a teenager, probably sixteen years old. It was like, "Okay, I am young and almost married, so I can show off with lots of clothes from England." Do you know what it means to get clothes from England in those days? I was so happy with myself that even before anyone could finish asking where my outfit was from, I would respond, "Oh yeah, it's from England."

Occasionally I would pinch my mum's clothes without her knowledge. I would go to her suitcase and take lovely blouses. It did not matter how big they were, we always found a way of tucking it in with the wrapper and taking pictures. So, my friends and I have gorgeous photos taken with everyone looking fantastic and rich, and no one could tell the clothes did not belong to us. In those days, we have a saying in pidgin English, "Borrow Borrow make me rich" meaning borrowing to enrich oneself. Sometimes, we swapped blouses with our friends to take pictures that we could then show off.

My fashion sense continued because I love clothes, and I enjoy dressing up. There is no limit to what I can spend on clothes and sometimes, this could be a problem. I live in a four-bedroom house, and one room is filled with my clothes. I think about giving them away, but then I think about my nieces and I think how much I would like to send the clothes to them and this ends up with me hoarding them. If I could find a way to up and send them to Nigeria, I would be very pleased. I am lucky that some of the expensive ones still fit, but maybe not as nice as before but I believe they still look nice on me. I guess the useful life of clothes also depends on the material they are made of. If you buy a good material or a good dress, they never go out of fashion. I enjoy spending whatever money I have on clothes. This is my vice. It is my weakness, and I have no regrets.

I do not have any particular time or season to buy clothes. If I walk into a shop at the moment and see something I like, I will buy it there and then. I do not have a budget for clothes either. I know the shops that I like. If I walk into Marks & Spencer, I am heading for their Peruna section. I like that section because they have intriguing outfits. Other 'mandatory' shops I shop at are Monsoon, Jacque Vert, Winsmoor, and Planets for their nice trouser. These are mainly the shops that I go to because I like their cuts and fittings.

You may be thinking about how a widow could spend a lot on clothes with four children and other financial commitments without running into debt. You see, there is a saying, "Cut your coat according to your size." and another "You can only put things on the ladder where you can reach." I work full time as a midwife, and for nurses, one good thing is that you can also "moonlight" that is, you can also do agency work. All the expenses come out of my earnings, including the mortgage and upkeep for the children.

I was already at the height of my profession from 1984 when I became a nursing sister. So, income from my main midwifery job was enough for my mortgage and other expenses. When I do agency work, that is my extra sweat and the earnings, I use to buy my clothes. So, I always have "cloth money." Unfortunately, the friends I have are just as bad as me when it comes to spending on clothes. When we go out, we would agree with my friends that we were not going to buy clothes. When we are out, I would suggest that we pop into a shop to browse without buying. As soon as I see something I like, I would say "Gosh that looks nice, I'll just try it on, but I won't buy it." But once I try it on, it just fits so nicely. I would ask my friends what they thought. They would say, "Kate that looks so beautiful, but you promised not to buy any clothes today." I would say yes, but I cannot leave this one. I have to buy it, and I would buy it.

I do not need to have a reason to go out and buy clothes. There is another shop I like to shop at these days. It is very lovely and calming for me. It is called TK Maxx. Sometimes, you find something different that nobody would have. A lot of people do not like going there because they do not have the patience to go through piles of clothes stacked together. But for me, as with all aspects of life, I have patience. That is probably why no matter what happens, I hardly get upset. In the time I should be upset, I would be working out how to surmount or tackle the issue.

I feel no shame or remorse because I do not have a clothing budget. I survived the loss of my husband, and I managed to bring up our four children, and they turned out fine. A lot of people know my children. As I am buying clothes for myself, if I see anything that might look nice on them, I buy as well.

Although my youngest daughter - the baby of the house likes clothes as much as I do, I am happy she doesn't buy clothes on impulse like me. I do not think she will mind my saying so. Talking about her, I just remembered something funny. Sometimes, when she sees me with a new outfit, she would say, "Oh mummy not again." I would say "oh no, I bought this a long time ago." Would you believe that sometimes I buy clothes and I either leave them in the boot of my car or somewhere tucked in my room? When I am ready to wear it, I will put it on, and she would ask, "Mummy when did you buy this?" Again, I will defend by saying "have you forgotten? I bought it a long time ago. I showed it to you remember?" Very quickly she would say "No mummy, you didn't show me." I would say, "Maybe you forgot. Anyway, how does it look?" She would say, "Mummy that looks nice on you".

If the outfit is stunning, I will show it to her straight away. Till now, when I buy clothes, even if I like it so much, and I think it is beautiful, I will leave it in my bag, or sometimes I hang it out. As I write this moment, I have one hanging out that I want to show her. If she says she does not like it, I will return it. That is how much I value her input.

I also love handbags. If I love one so much, you will be surprised that I will keep using that one until it starts showing signs of wear and tear, then I get on to the next one. I usually buy big, medium and small sized bags. So, when I go shopping, the two sections I go to are handbag and dress.

I am not as lucky with shoes because I am big size eight UK. That means that I do not usually find good, fashionable shoes that would fit me as they have to be wide fitting. Because I used to force my feet into shoes that were not right for me, I developed corn, and that has prevented me from wearing court shoes. I mostly wear mid-heel sandals when I dress up. I cannot help my feet size because that is purely down to genetics.

DANCING

After dressing up what should one do? For me, I like having a good time at parties. My good time means getting on the dance floor and boogying away. I love dancing. Anyone who knows me would know that I love dancing. I do not know when my love for dancing started. I would not say it started from my school. I think that by playing the kinds of music that I like, and when I realised that I could make a good move to each type of music it just developed. Like Shakespeare said, "If music be the food of love, play on." I think of music like my food, and I enjoy dancing. When I start dancing, I don't really care who is there, who is looking or who I am.

Let me tell you one funny thing that happened with regards to my dancing that I can never forget. Most of my friends know I love dancing and I don't care whoever is there as long as I am dancing to the music I like. Would you believe that when I was Mayor of Enfield, all my friends warned me, they said, "Kate no more dancing." Waoh!!!! This, I did not enjoy. I said, what? And they said, "Yes, you have to behave now. You have to behave like a mayor, no more dances." Guess what they did for me. I have a very good friend, who as soon as we get back after a mayoral function, would put on my kind of music and say "now you dance." It was like they were afraid of having a dancing Mayor, but there you go.

I agree with them in a way. You see when you are in a certain position; you change slightly to conform with the new you. That is why sometimes, people do not understand when people behave differently because they are in new positions. However, I do not think they should behave too differently to the point of being snobbish. That should never happen. People should not snob their friends and other people regardless of what position you hold or where you are.

Also with regards to my dancing during my tenure as mayor, I may be dancing and have people waiting for me, and they would probably say, "Come on let's go", and I'll say "Please wait till this music finishes." I think it might be embarrassing for them to tell me it is time to go in the middle of a dance because when we go to events, we have certain time limit especially if we have two to three events to cover in a day.

I thank God I have not had any dance disaster or committed any dance atrocity as of yet as I did with my fashion as a teenager. I don't think it would happen because the music these days are quite good. You can dance slow, medium, fast, or let loose.

Believe it or not, I like dancing to every kind of music especially the ones the youngsters are dancing to like P-Square. I love it, and I have no barrier. What about traditional music? Yes, I am equal to it. Would you believe that my granddaughter, Kamsi loves music and dancing too? When I tell people that Kamsi loves music and dancing, they say, "well we are not surprised after all, she has a dancing grandma." Music and dancing are social motilities, and they give me happiness. I believe that it is quite healthy as well.

Dancing, dressing up and going out; I love to do those things. I am not spending anybody's money. Even though I don't have much, but when it comes to clothes, I will find the money to buy them. I have enough savings because I don't drink alcohol, I don't drink tea, I don't drink coffee, and I don't smoke. My other vice is going to the gym. I like talking about health, not because I am a nurse, but because I believe I can see and feel what it has done for me.

HEALTHY LIFESTYLE

When I talk about health, I specifically mean the things you eat. People always say, "Kate you are always looking slim." I would say that I was not on a diet nor have I ever been. I watch what I eat because I believe that you are what you eat. If I am having our traditional food like *fufu*, I will make just precisely what I need, with plenty of soup. Sometimes, because the soup is tasty, you want to carry on eating and before you know it you have eaten the portion meant for three people. So, I make sure I take only the portion I am going to eat with plenty of soup.

In the mornings, I usually go for a light breakfast. I have one or two slices of brown bread and a cup of herbal tea. I don't eat white bread, it has to be wholemeal. If you ask my children, they will tell you that when mummy is not at home, we rejoice because that is when we go and buy white bread because we never have white bread when she is around. If I don't have herbal tea, I will have a mug of hot water, and that's breakfast.

I used to drink a lot of English tea. When my children used to live with me, they knew what time I returned home from work, and as soon as I come in a pot of tea and milk would be ready for me. I do not take sugar. Even if I am famished, I first have to sit and drink, sometimes topping up my tea. When I go to see my friends too, it is the same thing. Once I walk in, don't give me anything to eat as long as there is a pot of tea and milk, we can relax, chat and watch TV while I sip my tea and continue to top it up.

One day during Lent, before Easter I said to myself, "Lent is a period you should give up what you like best." All my friends knew I loved tea. So, in 2001, I gave up tea for Lent. Immediately after Easter Monday, the very next day, I was back to tea. Then I said, that was not too bad. I wanted to add coffee, but I only took one or two coffees in a week. The following year, I decided to do it again. I was able to complete it for the full forty days which included before and after Easter.

Then in 2003, I said to myself "I have to see how far I can go without tea and coffee after Lent without a specified time to stop." I am happy to announce to you that I still have not had coffee or tea since that time. So, since 2003 to date I have not had English tea or coffee. What it shows is number one, I am a determined person. Number two, I am disciplined. This is why when people say they cannot do certain things; I tell them that if they really want to do it, of course, they could because absolutely nothing is impossible.

My friends were quite puzzled on the whole giving up tea business. They kept asking why I stopped. Did the doctor ask you to? How did it happen? They never believed it came from me. They still think there must be a reason why the doctor stopped me from drinking tea. I told them there was absolutely nothing; I just stopped drinking tea because I gave it up during Easter 2003. I can always go back to drinking tea again if I wanted to, but I don't think it would ever happen. I drink plenty of hot water. I drink plenty of water, and if I want a bit of taste in my water, then I put some herbal tea made with herbal leaves. English tea is made with leaves as well, but it has caffeine. You can always get the caffeine free variant if you want.

For lunch, I have plenty of fruits. I think I developed this habit when I was working as a community midwife because we did not stop for lunch. So, when I am going out, I have different types of fruits in the car. If I am running a clinic and have a few minutes to spare I would just cut them up and eat. Sometimes, if I am working in the labour ward, I make my lunch with grated carrots, whole cabbage, and cucumber and mix them with tuna fish and very light salad dressing. Then I have it with toasted pitta bread, waoh!!! It is yummy, especially in summer; something light, enjoyable and healthy.

When I come home in the evening, I either had roasted potatoes with chicken or fish or either of them with vegetables. If I was having *fufu,* I would have a small portion of *garri* (cassava meal) mixed with oatmeal with plenty of soup. I like any soup, but I cook a lot of *egusi* soup because my children like it. Even now, when I prepare it, they come and take some. But now, I am running away from oil because of cholesterol. I love okra soup and bitter leaf soup. I love *egusi* soup, but there is a reason I am keeping away from it. I stay away because even though I feel 200% healthy, I have a family history of high cholesterol. Thus, obviously I have got high cholesterol, and I always have to keep an eye on it. I thank God that I do not have high blood pressure at all, and that is why I still touch wood. I am quite lucky because that is one of the things that would affect your health and the things you want to do.

I love all kinds of food. I cook a lot of English food as well. When the children were growing up, I cooked both Nigerian and English meals. The children love their fish and chips. I don't eat it, but I don't deny them either. I even cook Italian, things like spaghetti and pasta. I also cook potatoes; I boil, roast or mash them. Although I cook all these foods, I don't eat all of them. I think the only time I eat more than I should is when we go out to parties. You know you usually party with your friends, and you end up eating at odd hours, even at midnight. That would never happen at my house. In my house, by 6 or 7 pm I would have finished eating. If I feel like something else later, I go for something light.

One other thing I love is popcorn. Sometimes when I am hungry, instead of going for anything else I go and make some popcorn, lightly salted. I like making it myself because the ones you buy from the shop are either filled with sugar or salt. Popcorn is one of the things I enjoy eating, and I can eat it anytime.

Apart from popcorn, when it comes to Nigerian food, my favourite is yam. You can cook it anyhow. Everybody back in Nigerian; my sisters-in-law and siblings all know that I love yam.

I do not know if I have any favourite non-Nigerian food. I love roasted potatoes, but I don't like mashed or boiled potatoes. My roasted potatoes have to be served with fish. I love salmon. I always make sure that I have salmon in my freezer. As for the vegetables, any type of vegetable is fine with me.

KEEPING FIT

I love going to the gym. Years ago, I used to go to the gym about 2-3 times a week. I could not go more than three times a week because of work and everything else. I try to work out at home, but it is not quite as easy because you are always distracted by either telephone calls or some chores. Before you know it, you are in front of the TV. I am a member of the local gym at the Leisure Centre in Enfield.

I also did yoga as well as Pilates. In 2008, I went on a Hawaiian cruise. The first cruise I went on was in 2006, and I did not take notes. The second one I went to, I was more aware of what was happening. While the ship docked at Honolulu, I came up on the deck, and there was a swimming pool. Things you never knew and or would ever believe if you did not see for yourself. I watched people diving in and out, swimming as it was a very sunny and glorious day. All I could do was sit at the Jacuzzi, and after bubbling, I would come out. It did not quite feel the same. I said to our group of ladies, "Girls, you know what? When I go back to England, I am going to learn how to swim." Those who could not swim all agreed to take lessons as well.

So, when we got back to England, I went to register for swimming lessons at Edmonton Leisure Centre with some of the other ladies. It was a 13-week course. On lesson days, the ladies would say "Kate, oh I just came back from work. I'm too tired, can we go next week?" I would say "no, no I'm going." So, I went on my own, after all, we all paid separately.

I continued learning, and then one day I said to the tutor, "I can't float, I find myself sinking, and maybe I'm too heavy for the water." She said to me, "You know what Kate, come. " She pointed to a lady swimming and said, "You see that lady coming there, sit down and watch her." So, I sat and watched the lady. She was swimming like a fish, I tell you. And when she got to the end and got out, I screamed inside, "Geees!" This lady was four times my size. The course tutor said to me, "Have you got anything to say to me?" I said "no." I had nothing to say. That was when I said to myself, "Yes you can swim." She said to me, "Don't depend on the lesson. When you've got time come to the water and mess around." I said, "Okay, I'll do that."

So, whenever I finish early from work, I would go straight to the pool, and on my day off as well. I would practice for a little bit up to where it says "non-swimmers not allowed" and I would turn back. I did this regularly. Then one day, I asked myself, "These people swimming to the deep end, have they got two heads?" As I have been told and I have seen that I was not too heavy to float. That day, I decided that I was going to the end of the pool. So, I started, and I kept paddling. It took me a good half hour to get to the end. By the time I got to the deep end, some people had done forty laps. Nothing could take away my joy that I completed the lap even though it took me half an hour. Then, my time was up for that day. On my way home, I thought to myself that this swimming business is hard, but I would not give up, and I did not.

I continued practising. The day I did two laps, I came home, and I could not wait for my daughter to come home. By now, it was just both of us living in the house. The moment she walked in, I called her, "Chinny come, guess what? I did two laps today." She was happy for me and said, well-done mummy. I was very pleased with myself, and I appreciated her encouragement. So, I continued practising and gradually increased the laps. The day that I did about six laps, I came home and sat on the chair. I could not get up. All my body was aching. I said to her "I think I have done too much." The following week, I cut down the laps and went back to four, then built it up again. Now I do 32-40 laps in 45 minutes. It may not count as much, but for me, I could not be happier.

I promised myself, and I have been swimming three times a week for a while now. I swim on Mondays, Wednesdays and Fridays. If I miss any day because of engagements that I could not move, then I will go the next day. I also aim to do no less than 32 laps because it takes me between half an hour to forty-five minutes to accomplish. I am quite happy with that, and it has been terrific. Swimming is now my main exercise, especially now that I have back problems, one of the occupational hazards of the nursing profession. When I go to the gym, I go just for yoga or Pilates. I have two friends I met at the pool; we call ourselves "swim friends." We also go out together for meals or cinema. When one of these friend's son got married, the atmosphere was electric. I had never been to an Indian wedding before, so it was a fantastic event to look forward to. I observed families and friends spending many evenings eating and enjoying, before the actual wedding day. I tucked into different freshly made Indian cuisine. Our hands were decorated with henna and it was a beautiful wedding the next day. I thought Igbo wedding was very demanding and sometimes complicated, especially the traditional marriage. But you know what? I was wrong. Indian weddings are very expensive, and on observation, you do not need an accountant to tell that it costs an arm and a leg. The actual wedding rite was going on and on and on, in a lot of stages. Anyway, it is a memorable day for the young couple, so we should not complain.

RELATIONSHIP

Many people wonder why I did not remarry, and there was a particular reason for that. When you have children, it is not that easy because there are many things you have to put into consideration. You have to consider the person who is coming in; is that person coming with less baggage? That is, is that person single, with or without children? Are his children going to like your children? Are your children going to like his children? The main barrier was would your children like him. You will find with four children, one may like him, one will not, and others may be indifferent. It was such a delicate area, and it does not help you at all. Also, I think it is not a very good thing for nurses when it comes to a relationship.

Nurses are very independent, strong will-powered and can be on their own. Sometimes, you look at relationships, and you will find that some people want relationships because they want company or they need someone to help them financially, and this happens more in America where many men want to marry nurses. For me, I did not need anyone to help me financially. This is not to say that if it comes, one would say no, but that would not be part of the reason to build up a relationship, because I was fairly comfortable financially. I did not have much money, but I did not lack.

Some people have plenty of money and do not know what to do with it, but I am not in that category. I am in the group where if I go out to the shop and I find something that I like, I would go for it as long as I could afford it, just like the saying, "Cut your coat according to your size." I don't go shopping at Harrods because I cannot afford Harrods. I can go to another high street shop where I can buy nice things that fit me that when I wear them, I look like a million dollars as far as I am concerned, and I can walk with my head held high.

As for marrying for companionship, I still think when you are bringing up children, it is tough to juggle both; trying to please the children and your companion. When the children are grown and have left home, then you might start to think you need that companionship. My children have all left home now, and I think this is the time I need that companionship. But it has to come freely. It is not something I will actively look for. If it happens, fine. As for me to go look for it, I am too busy for that.

I also think that it is something you have to think twice and envisage the outcome for the sake of the children.. Also, I had more than one child. If it was just one child, you could talk to one child. But with four of them, if you spoke to one, he or she may say okay, but the others might say, "Ermm she's left us" or "she doesn't care about us." One child is enough to make their sibling feel like mummy has abandoned them. It is very sad what women go through when they are widowed.

I think it is easier for the men because obviously, he would be encouraged by his friends to remarry as soon as possible with the inference that he needs a woman to help look after the children. But for the woman, it is not that easy. Although I dated but it was not easy.

If any relationship were to happen now, I am 200% sure I would not want marriage. I will take the companionship. All I think these days is me, me, me! So often we spend our time pleasing others, be it our boss, family or friends. After working in the National Health Service for forty years and raising four good citizens, I believe it is in order for me to think about the rest of my life. This is the time to let my hair down, do something new, to switch into the mode for exploring the limits of my inner child. Dance like no one is watching and if it was possible, drop in on a local karaoke bar, sing without holding back and be adventurous. To be comfortable and to do things that please me, I have organised my house to accommodate my mobility as I grow older. I have a four-bedroom house, and without moving out of the house, I have downsized to just enough space for me when I come home. If I have a friend, he can come, chat and watch TV, etc. but marriage is a no, no. With the same token people say "never say never" so I should stick with, no, no, but never say never.

My children are grown now, and they have their relationships. When you are a mother, you think of what is more important; your children or your relationship? I think you would always put your children first, especially when you are raising them alone in a foreign country and you don't want them to go off the rail. If your children derailed, you would find people putting one and two together and calling it six. So, it is imperative that whatever you do, you have to be very discreet because you want to respect your children, and of course yourself. There should be a relationship of trust between you and your children.

With age comes the understanding and appreciation of your most important asset, your health.

- Oprah Winfrey

Chapter Thirteen

TOP SIX ATTRIBUTES

My top six attributes that have helped shape my life are patience, discipline, wisdom, determination, not worrying (calmness) and believing in myself.

PATIENCE

A lot of things have happened, and I have watched people especially women who are mothers and are supposed to be role models, behave in manners not worthy of parents. I discovered that even if I did not have the patience in me at the moment it was needed, I still find it very difficult to display or react unreasonably. I do receive verbal abuse directly and sometimes indirectly from my fellow women, but I have skin, which is very thick and impermeable to the abuse of unruly women. Patience is the key. A Leader is a servant, and if you lack patience, you will have no wisdom. You see, I do not understand why women behave badly and see everything as a competition, instead of emulation.

For example, something happened to me in 2016, where a woman of over fifty tried to stop me from entering a public building. She was ranting and puffing up and down the stairs and even called me by the simplest name anybody could call me; that is Kate. I am much older than a lot of the people I associate with, but they do not know it because of the way I have taken care of myself. I looked at this woman, and inside me, I thought "how dare you?"

I believe any other person would have screamed, and there would have been an exchange of angry words with a lot of noise. However, I had the patience and self-control to just observe. I observed this woman working herself up and down. If any reasonable person witnessed what was happening, I am sure they would have wondered why I did not offer a counter response to the woman. It took patience and wisdom to conduct myself at that moment and of course in similar situations at other times. It is in moments like that that if you do not have patience, you will make mistakes because you reacted too quickly.

WISDOM

In organisations where you find yourself as the Chairperson, President or Coordinator, you will come across one woman or a group of women who would want to blame you for anything that did not go their way. If you are the coordinator or president, it is silly for you to lose it and start exchanging words. A leader in any organisation is a servant and must be prepared to absorb insults and abuse directly or indirectly. You are supposed to be the leader there, and you cannot react, you just let them carry on. I want to borrow the words of the English that says "Silence is the best answer to a fool." You have to excuse me as I am just quoting something and not that I have called anyone a fool.

At the time you are silent, you have made them realise that they are acting like the fools in the above saying because you have not answered back as they expected. But as soon as you answer back, you have lost your edge. You need to use wisdom to control yourself and find the appropriate time to address the issue. If you miss the appropriate time, you will end up exchanging words. By exchanging words, you would bring yourself down to their level and in the process lose the respect you have worked so hard to gain.

So, it is very important that you know how to control yourself and you develop through experience. It is also not by you saying it but through your actions. You don't go about saying to people that you have got wisdom. You don't. Instead, let people be the judge of that. People should say she has got wisdom. By applying wisdom, you are doing something positive not to escalate the issue. You choose the appropriate time to discuss and solve the problem. A lot of people have told me that I speak and do things with wisdom. All I know is that I am doing things as they come to my head.

NOT WORRYING (CALMNESS)

Firstly, can anybody tell me the benefits of worrying? Would worrying solve your problems? That is what I would like to know. If worrying is not going to solve your problem, why worry? You see people come to me and ask, "Kate how did you manage to bring up these children? How did you manage all of the boys and girls and they've all gone to the University?" I usually say, "Well if I'd worried about what I was going to do, how would that have helped." I always add this analogy that I also use for people who are envious of others. The analogy is God has given us a specific time to achieve or do something. If you have five minutes and within that five minutes God said that you should use two minutes to eat your food, and you could use another two minutes to hurry up and get dressed, and you use the remaining one minute to reach your destination. If you deviate from any; it is either you did not dress up, eat your food or get to your destination because you have the specified time that God has created for you not to worry or to envy someone.

We all have specific times and any time wasted can never be regained, so why waste time worrying? Would worry solve the problem? No. Would worry help you out? No. Would worry regain whatever you have lost? No. Worry would only make things worse. I don't believe in worrying. I believe in using the time people spend worrying to think about how to solve the problem.

Here is an example, at the moment I have got some people doing some work for me in my house. I came home one day and everywhere was very dusty. I said to the lead person, "Ah, ah! You told me it's not going to be dusty, but it's very dusty that I can't even breathe." He just stood looking at me. Then I said, "You know what, why don't you open the windows." I could have started screaming, "Oh my God, everywhere is dusty. What should I do?" Instead, I calmly proposed a solution when I realised that they did not know what to do. I even told them that the dust was not good for their health too. So, I did not just talk about myself, but I have reflected it to them about their health and opening windows. For me I have achieved what I wanted; I told them about the dust and opening the windows, and it should help them next time. I then asked the lead person, "Next time you come to work here, and you know it is going to be even dustier what is going to happen?" He said, "Don't worry Aunty, we'll cover things." I said I would wait and see.

I could have handled the incident the way I did, or I could have just started worrying about it, but what would it solve? Is it going to settle the dust? No, the dust would still be there, and the workmen still have to work. The important thing is to wait and see.

DETERMINATION

Determination is amazing. I think determination is one of my best value and attribute. After I lost my husband, I focused on my children. But there was one course that I wanted to study and it was Law. Obviously, for somebody with four children, a full-time job and a mortgage to take care of, it was not going to be easy. However, I remained determined. I said to myself; "You see this Law degree, I am going to study it." How would you study Law with your four children and a full-time job? It is a matter of working it out to see how I could do it. So, I just carried on with what I was doing while waiting for the right time. I attended all my children's parent evenings, noting their progress and making sure where I noted where they needed improvement. I worked in partnership with the teachers for a better outcome.

As soon as my youngest turned eight, I decided that the time was right for me to study Law, but first, I had to apply. When I applied at the University of North London, I remember what the female lecturer said to me. I can never forget her. Three lecturers interviewed me, and the lady amongst them said "You've got your nursing qualification; you're a registered nurse and midwife, why do you want to do this? You've got four children, and you're a widow, who's going to look after the children?" I said I had always wanted to be a lawyer. I got my daughter to study law, but it had not filtered into my body. I also encouraged my brother to study Law; he is a barrister now practising in Nigeria. But it was not the same. I did not still feel complete, and that was why I wanted to study it myself.

They asked me to go home and think about it, and I said okay. Then they told me that I had all the qualifications for them to accept me and they could even give me one year off because of my other certificates. That meant that instead of five years, I could study the course for four years part-time. Waoh! For me that is a big bonus, one whole year off, this even made me more determined. But then I still had a high mountain to climb, and that was convincing the lecturers that I could study all the law subjects despite my unbelievable responsibilities.

Two weeks later, they wrote to me and asked if I had decided what to do. I said yes, I had made up my mind, I was going to study Law, and there was no going back. They said okay, fine, and they confirmed my admission into the University. My lectures were on Monday and Wednesday evenings. I had Fridays off from my midwifery work. I used the opportunity to go in to University to do extra studies and meet and work with the young people.

So, that is the determination that I'm talking about. Even though my brother and my daughter studied Law, I still did not feel complete, and so I had to do it myself. I was determined to study Law, and I did it and got what I wanted. For me, obtaining a Law degree was like winning the lottery.

I do not doubt that going to University and having the opportunity to study with young people helped me to develop a soft spot for them. They had great respect for me, but they could not fathom why a busy single mother with four children and a full-time demanding job would embark on such a tedious study for a Law degree.

I made a 2:2 just like some of the young people and some of them even made a third class. It just shows that in life, nothing is impossible, if you are determined and articulate, you can reach your potential. The key is; believe in yourself, be determined and keep away from friends who are pulling you down.

Although I worked hard to get my law degree, I still could not give up midwifery. I was so enthused with delivering babies that I could not let go. Some of my colleagues have their Law firms now, but I have no regrets. I remain thankful to the Almighty Father above for giving me the ability to contribute towards the world population by aiding mothers during birth and supporting families. Nonetheless, I still feel that studying for a Law degree was one of the best things I did for myself. I finally got what I always wanted. I made use of my legal knowledge within my maternity unit. Also, I became the Royal College of Midwives Steward - that is, their Union Representative. I was able to support and assist my colleagues. I used my legal knowledge to review some of the notes especially when there is a query of medical negligence within our care. I really enjoyed doing that. I'm glad that I made use of my knowledge in the most satisfying way. I believe my midwifery career and legal knowledge contributed immensely to my interest in politics.

All my children are always determined because they knew how determined I had to be in bringing them up and in making sure that they were well provided for and on the right path. I reminded them of how I was able to study Law while having a full-time career and being both a mum and dad to them. Now, I tell them that what they have achieved today is not the end and that there are many other things they can add to their career; something they can do on the side like they have seen me do, but maybe on a different level.

I am a community person, and I love being out there, working in the community. I have been working in the Enfield community long before I got into the Nigerian community and in recognition of my service in the community; I was awarded an **Honorary Freeman of the Borough of Enfield.**

The inscription on the certificate says it is awarded, "In recognition for her long and valuable service to the community, for her outstanding contribution to the voluntary sector and as an expression as the highly esteemed in which she's held."

Apart from the certificate issued to me, the title also has other privileges. Number one, if any civic event is organised in the Borough, everyone with Honorary Freeman of the Borough is invited. This is unlike serving as a Councillor that all privileges stop once your term ends. With this title, I am always on their list until I have passed on. Many years ago, when this title came into effect, it was said that people with Honorary Freeman of the Borough title could graze their sheep anywhere in the Borough. They could also go into any pub and get free drinks. Anyway, I did not miss the free drink offer as I don't drink alcohol.

DISCIPLINE

I am a disciplined person. An example is how I gave up tea and how I learnt to swim. The friends whom I enrolled with to attend swimming lessons used to tell me that they could not come because they were tired after work. Guess what? Those friends of mine still cannot swim till today. When they came up with excuses of being tired after work or that they've got cold etc. I just said you know what, I've decided so I'm going to do it and I just carried on. Once I say this is what I want to do, I will do it. If I decide to achieve ten goals today, I will do exactly that. I am always determined with where I want to go to except if it is not God's will for me. But if it comes down to me to try and get there myself, I'm very determined and disciplined.

I am also very good with my time management. Time management is critical if you want to be successful because there are only twenty-four hours a day for everyone, and if you want to achieve anything that day, then you need to manage your time properly because you do not get extras.

BELIEVE IN YOURSELF

I am a very positive person, and I believe that nothing is impossible. I also believe that I can do anything, and I think that everybody should have that belief about themselves too. If you believe in yourself, then that is one hurdle to success sorted. When you start doubting yourself, that is, when all the things you could have done right start feeling impossible. Then you begin to wonder why you have not achieved your goals; it is because your negative auras fill your head. I am of the opinion that 1% negativity is enough to annul 99% positivity, so if you ever doubt yourself, that is it. If you have a quibble in mind, and your mind is saying, shall I or shall I not? Or can I or can I not? You need to be mindful of your thoughts at such times. I am very mindful of the things that I do. To quote Sheridan-Williams "A quick trick to promote calm is to find something blue in your surroundings, whether it is the pool, a calm sky view or ocean waves outside your window. Stare at it for 60 seconds, taking in three deep breaths and getting lost in the moment. The blue will promote calm while the deep breathing will help you focus on the now." Cordwell agrees and said, "Short mindfulness meditation or self-hypnosis recordings can do wonders to promote deep relaxation which can stay with you."

We are at the mercy of social media these days. Trying to live up to the expectations of the perfect selfie and photoshop celebrities on Instagram and other social media platforms creates unrealistic pressures, which will severely challenge your ability to enjoy yourself and cause one unnecessary stress. It is important to post the pictures that make you happy and add meaning to your life, forget about the numbers of likes and shares. Looking to others to make you happy will inevitably only leave you unfulfilled.

With that said, you may recall what happened the first time in my life that I doubted myself. Yes, I did doubt myself when I applied for the seat of MP. The reason was that I had not attended the induction training necessary for the role before making the application. Also, it had never crossed my mind to run for the post of MP. If it had ever crossed my mind, obviously I would have had some belief that I could do it. But because I was not prepared and I did not believe that I could do it, I did not reach my goal. Obviously, you also need people around you to encourage you to go for higher posts. They believe you can achieve things, even those things that have never crossed your mind. It is essential that you always have such people around you. I have my children around me to "Say, yes mum, you can!" With their push, I say, "Okay let's get on with it." I could not believe how far I went. As I mentioned earlier, if it were a race to win a medal, I would have gotten the bronze medal. So, for me, it was still a huge success.

Believe in yourself. You are braver than you think, more talented than you know, and capable of more than you imagine.

–Roy T. Bennett

Chapter Fourteen

PASSING DOWN THE ATTRIBUTES

I guess it is highly expected of me to raise my children with my top six attributes. It is really just a matter of them looking at you, their parent and the things you have done. Some of them might like to emulate you, and some of them might like to leave it till later. If you were to ask my youngest about the things she is doing and where she got her courage, determination and things like that from, she would definitely tell you "Oh, my mummy is my role model; my mummy never gave up." It is nice to know that they observed and saw how I struggled and that they are proud of what I did and how I got there.

Now my youngest daughter has a baby, and she comes to me at times panting with exhaustion saying, "Mummy I don't know how you did it. I've got only one, and I'm tired." At times I want to say, "I did it with four of you so you too can manage with just one." Then I thought no, no, no, we are all separate individuals. Inasmuch as she came from me, we are still different individuals, and you must never compare yourself with other people. You could say that you would like to emulate and do things like them but do not go making the type of comparison that is going to hurt their feelings. You should know the types of comparison that would help you move forward.

I have raised my children to appreciate that we were raised from different backgrounds and environments. For example, back home in Nigeria especially in the rural area, children wore clothes until it was really worn out, but here in the UK, it is not the same. So, I always remind them that my nieces and nephews do not have as many clothes as they have. My children know that if they do not like any of their clothes anymore, they do not just throw them out. If the clothes are woolly and would be too warm for Nigeria, we give them to charity here in England. If they are of light material, I send them home. So, they have learnt that we were brought up from different environments; different ways and our lives are much different.

NOT WORRYING (CALMNESS)

An example of not worrying is when they were growing up and getting into relationships. Some of my children were quite happy to discuss their relationships with me and seek advice. As every parent knows, it is relationship matters that our children do not want to discuss with their parents, and this you cannot fault them. When they decide to talk, it is the best thing any parent can wish for.

Let your daughters be your friends, your sisters, your companions. Through this, there is team building, trust and you the parent, become the counsellor, the mother, aunty, friend and big sister. We must let go of the type of barriers of the upbringing we had with our parents when we were growing up. Anyway, the culture in the United Kingdom has cancelled out that type of upbringing. I still believe strongly that there are some of our culture that made us who we are, which we must hold onto, that will help our children to grow, remember their roots and remain respectful to their parents and elders. You do not lose parental respect because you are a friend of your child, rather it brings you closer.

At times I question myself and wonder if I am doing the right thing to help my children to develop their education and solve their problems. I know the responsibility as a parent is enormous and often you can feel like you are not doing enough to really create harmony in your family life. In bringing up my children as a single parent, I realised that we are all sensitive in one or more areas, and when you know how to work with that respectfully, everything changes, regardless of culture and beliefs.

I remember when one was complaining about a relationship not working, I comforted her by telling her that the relationship was definitely not for her because if it were, things would have worked out. I told her to let it go. At the same time, I reminded her that it may still come back to worry her as to why it did not work out, but she should remember what mummy said that if it were meant to be, it would not have failed; because we cannot see through our future, only God can. God saw that it was not for her and He found a way to resolve and dissolve it. We cannot erase the past, but we can change the future. My ultimate aim was to provide emotional and social support to my children so that they are better able to manage their emotions and relationships within the school and external settings. I believe that support and approach made a lot of positive difference in bringing up my children. On the other hand, the same method might not work for siblings; this is because human beings are unique even if you are of the same mother and father.

BELIEVE IN YOURSELF

My children believe in themselves, especially my youngest daughter. I think her attitude is similar to mine. When she was studying for her Master's degree she was talking about photography and buying a camera and to take pictures of people with, and I thought to myself, "I don't think so." She asked if I could help her financially to get the camera she wanted. I had my doubts, but I trusted her. She eventually did it. Now and then, she would say to me, "You remember that time when I wanted to buy a camera, and I wanted to take pictures, and you responded to me negatively, and that was like, you can't do it." And I would say, "Yes." I suppose I doubted her because I did not believe she could do it.

I know that all my children are intelligent and coped well in school, but I thought that my youngest child needed a little bit of a push. For some reason, she had this will power to studying that when she went to university, she said to me, "Mummy I'm going to make a 2:1."

I have always taught if you are determined and you believe in yourself, you can make it. Where there is a will, there is a way. Then I just said to her, why not? She made a 2:1, and was like, "I told you." I said, yes, you were determined and you believed in yourself that you could do it. You could, and you made it. With her 2:1, she went on to study for her Masters. For me as a mother, I wanted to give everything to make a difference in their lives so that they could move in the direction of growth in their education.

WISDOM

The dictionary defines wisdom as, the quality of having experience, knowledge, and good judgement; the quality of being wise. Some say wisdom is the body of knowledge and experience that develops within a specified society or period. It is also defined as the fact of being based on sensible or wise thinking.

As for wisdom, my children have all left home. I believe they must be using wisdom to achieve some of the things they are doing. Sometimes, when you are not with them, you believe they are doing the right things especially when you have raised them well. But then again, we were not born with wisdom. We acquire wisdom as we get older. I believe that wisdom comes with age, and it has really been a blessing to me in dealing with some of the issues and people I meet as the days go by, especially women. In life, if you lose everything, don't lose your character and dignity. This is my guide. I have come across women of many characters; women who find me a threat for some reason best known to them.

DISCIPLINE

My children are quite disciplined because I have instilled it in them and they recognise the things you can achieve when you discipline yourself, and also what could go wrong when you are out of control. I believe if you can put yourself together, that would help you to discipline yourself in so many ways. It is just about planning. Proper planning prevents poor performance; you have to plan the little things to make the big things easier. In essence, life gets more comfortable. I believe that planning my health fitness got me where I am today. When I am discussing healthy living, I first of all talk about discipline, before I talk about exercise. No matter how busy I am, I always plan exercise into my schedule. I plan everything, juggling my time and movement, and that is without jotting anything down on paper.

People say managing makes the difference, especially time management. You have to first plan, and then you manage. If you plan right, everything else falls into place. I believe parents are the first role models children will come across. Promoting good family values and reorienting our children to inculcate good values will reduce indiscipline, crime and other vices. A model parent teaches the children the thematic words such as honesty, conscience, integrity, respect, etc. Sometimes we parents forget that our children observe every movement we make, what we say and how we say it. Regrettably, some parents believe in do as I say but not as I do. Unfortunately for them, actions speak louder than words. Our children copy us in all aspects because they believe the adult is always right. At times, we wonder why some children are rude to adults; it is because they see their parents or adults quarrel and get confrontational in meetings and community groups, which is very sad. If adults cannot control themselves, what do you expect from a young person who is trying to find his or her footing in the community?

I was raised to believe that excellence
is the best deterrent to racism or sexism.
And that's how I operate my life.

- Oprah Winfrey

Chapter Fifteen

FAITH & RELIGION

Faith and religion have played a massive part in my life not only because I was from a very staunch Catholic background, but also I think it has helped me to overcome and achieve things in my everyday family life. It helped me to successfully raise my family because I immersed myself fully in my faith. I did not just go to church; I became very active as well. We were out there in the church on Sundays, and that has played a massive role with Chinelo if not all of my children.

With children, you impact in some areas of their lives, but they still have to choose who they are. When it comes to religion, you have to be open-minded. As we grow, we evaluate and decide which one we want to practice. You trying to instil certain aspects of religion in your children is okay when they are young, but when they grow up, you have to let go. As adults, they are on their own; they are saving their souls, so you let go and allow them to carry on. My children carried on with what they wanted to practice, and those who wanted to carry on with the Catholic faith carried on. The most important thing is not hurting others with whatever religion you choose to practice.

I am very active in my Catholic faith, helping out in the church. There are numerous Catholic women organisations which I am also a part of. I also officiate in the church as well. I am one of the Eucharistic Ministers - that is one of those who help in giving out Holy Communion in the church. We get special training, and every year we go for a retreat and observe some prayers. I still maintain that because I think it has helped me.

TESTING MY FAITH

I think when people go through bereavement that is when they are shaken. This is when they ask; "Where is God? If there is God why should this happen to me?" If you can overcome that, then it is good. Some people might not be able to overcome, and this leads them to change their faith immediately. There will be people from other religions coming to you to say that you will be better off in their religion. They came to me when I was bereaved and told me exactly that. I just gave them the audience and listened to their preaching, and that was it.

I know I asked God some questions. I asked; "I have got four children, why have I been left alone to look after them; two people can't manage one why do I have to manage four?" As someone raised in Nigeria, I was taught not to question God. When I remembered it, I stopped questioning God. Also, in January 1979 when I had a cot death in the hospital for would have been baby number three born full term, good weight, and no problems, but the next thing I knew, he was gone. I asked questions. I did not get any answers to the questions I asked though. I remember my mum telling me not to ask God questions because that was the belief back home in Nigeria. They believe that when you ask questions, you doubt God and that there is no need for the questions because God allowed whatever it is to happen. So, I stopped asking questions and had to accept what happened and started thinking about ways of coping and overcoming it.

My coping and overcoming strategy was to believe that God would not give you a burden you could not bear. I saw the passing of my husband as a cross that was given to me, that I had to carry. I had to carry it carefully with patience and dignity. I had to carry it without hate but with love, and I had to carry it without questioning God anymore. Sometimes, I complain that the cross is heavy and it is wearing me down. I used to get counselling, and I remember saying to the lady on the phone, "It is very heavy, I can't carry it anymore." I told her that today was worse than yesterday and I thought it was supposed to get lighter, but yesterday seemed lighter than today.

I believed in that cross, and I could feel its weight. With time, it became lighter, and as it grew lighter, I thought back, and I said: "Yes I shouldn't have asked questions, but rather believed in what I was told that God doesn't give you a cross heavier than you could carry." We have this saying in Igbo, and it goes, "*Chukwu adi ebunyegi ibu kaliligi*"

The Counselling I had when my husband passed away really helped, and I wish I had it when I had the cot death. I remember going back to work after the cot death, and I burst out crying on one of my nightshifts. When my colleagues asked me what the matter was, I told them that none of them had asked me anything about the baby and it was like nothing happened. Then they said, "We're so sorry Kate we didn't know what to do. We thought maybe it might be opening old wound if we'd asked." I said no, you could have talked about it. If I had counselling, I don't think I would have had that kind of outburst.

I used my experience of cot death at work. It helped me to talk to other women who had experienced cot deaths. When I tell them that it happened to me, they would say, "What? We never thought it happened to midwives as well." I would say, "Yes, midwives are human beings, and this happens to them too." They'd then say, "Oh, thank you for sharing this with me. It really made me feel better because I've been wondering if it's something that I'd done and that's why it happened to me." I would continue encouraging them by saying that it had nothing to do with what they had or not done, but they should just believe the way I believed that it was God's wish that it would happen.

I did not just support women who had experienced cot death; I also supported and still support widows. I say to them if I survived, you will survive. I like visiting and talking to them. The last one I spoke with was a young mother. In her mum's presence, I said to her, "You are lucky your mum is here. When mine happened, my mum was not here. I could not even bring my mum over for a few months, but your mum is staying with you." I continued by saying to her that if I survived, she could survive too. I felt that she just had an instant rapport with me straight away. I could tell that she felt that I understood what she has been through and where she was coming from. She said, "I'm worried about two children, but yours were four." Then her mum told her about a nice aunty of hers who could help with her children.

When we look back on all the perils through which we have passed and at the mighty foes that we have laid low and all the dark and deadly designs that we have frustrated, why should we fear for our future? We have come safely through the worst.

- Winston Churchill

Chapter Sixteen

FAMILY & FRIENDS CONTRIBUTION

MR ARINZE EZEASOR – Brother

Kate Anolue is my elder sister and having her as my sister is a great privilege. During the Nigerian civil war, we were still quite young. She was about 15 years old but she did a lot of little businesses to help our family. She trekked more than 15-20 kilometres to buy peanuts (called groundnuts in Nigeria) and then prepare them for sale. The next day she would trek another 15-20km to go and sell those peanuts. She also sold rice as well. If she had not done these, I don't know how my parents would have brought us up. It was because of her efforts my parents did not lose any of us and nor did we suffer from malnutrition called kwashiorkor during the war. She took proper care of us then and even continued when she left for England. In fact, she raised all of us her younger siblings. She is the kind of sister that I would always like to have, anytime, anyplace, in this life and the next. Whenever you have a problem, and you call her, she would listen to you. She would try as much as she could to help. She also helped us with our education. My whole family; my parents and my siblings hold her in high esteem and give her utmost respect because of her invaluable love and support to all of us.

I am really not sure where and how she got her entrepreneurial attributes from, but I noticed that she watched how our cousins and others older than her did things and helped out. She also helped our mother manage her market stall.

I believe that my sister is really blessed because it seems that everything she touches turns into gold. During the civil war, she would cook soup and *garri* and take them to a place called *Awa* in Orumba North Local Government. *Awa* from our place is about 15 kilometres. She sold up very quickly because her food was delicious. She met a woman there who liked her, and they became friends. The woman saw a little girl struggling, and she liked her and told her she could stay in her house. The woman saw that my sister came a long way to *Awa*, so she allowed her to stay at her place so that she would not have to trek so far and so she could cook more food too. This helped to expand her business.

Why I said that she helped our parents a lot was because, after her business, she would buy things we needed at home. She would also give our parents money to spend on us. This made us all very happy during the war. She knew that parents loved children who are interested in helping to bring up their siblings, something not enough people do. My sister is not selfish. Some people in the village were happy to see how industrious she was and some were even jealous of our parents because they felt our parents were lucky to have her. She believed in business and herself. She did not wait for people to do things for her because that was the type of person she is. She always planned ahead. She knows what she wants, and she can work for it.

I remember when she left Nigeria and did her nursing profession in London. Inasmuch as our father pushed her into nursing, she ended up loving it and excelling at it. However, she still went on to study Law she always wanted. She did all these after she was widowed at a young age, with four children to raise alone. Nonetheless, she was still able to train all her children to graduate level.

I believe her seeing all of us her little ones whom she left behind really makes her happy. We, the little ones she left behind have now grown up and are married with children. You know what though, she still sees us as her little ones; she never believed that we are adults.

She gets upset when people lie to her, and she is unhappy when people are being lazy. When we were growing up, she made sure we took our education seriously. If she catches you playing when you should be studying, she got upset and told you off. If she sends you on an errand or asks you to do a chore and you prefer to play instead, she would not be happy with you. If she found out that you were involved in a fight with other children, she would tell you off and advise you to concentrate on your education because that was the best thing to do. We learnt a lot from her as our elder sister.

The top three things I learnt from her are, to be honest in whatever I'm doing, to have focus, and to know what I want in life and plan for it.

My sister is very kind, and she has a lot of friends. I know she likes helping people and whatever you ask from and of her, she would gladly give if she has it.

She has invited me to London at least three times. When I think of her success in London, I am speechless. When she became Mayor of Enfield, I was present at her inauguration ceremony. At the event, I kept thinking about how she became Mayor after seeing all the white population in Enfield. I felt that she must be a special person to have become so successful. I did not know exactly how to feel; everything seemed like a miracle. I could not believe that a Nigerian could achieve all that.

My proudest moment about my sister has to be on her inauguration as the Mayor of Enfield. Seeing her there, getting all the attention and greeting people, all I could do was watch and think wow, is that really my sister or is that someone else?

We really love our sister, and we know that she really love us, and we would like her to recognise that we are adults now, because she still treats us like we are babies.

I honestly cannot do anything without consulting her. She loves all of us; me, my children and my wife. We cannot do without her because we know that in anything, she would tell you the truth. Where and when you need support, she will give it. My sister is just too good, and we will always be grateful to her.

CHINELO ANYANWU – Daughter

My mother is a very loving person. From a young age, if she sees that I or my siblings have a passion for something that might not be the norm, as in the whole African sense where typically some parents push you towards being a doctor, a lawyer or those kinds of career paths; she would always encourage us. She was and still supports us in any area of our lives. To make sure we are happy doing what we love, she would ask us what we are passionate about, whether it was extra-curricular activities or other areas, she would push us to achieve our dreams. My mum is obviously a stickler for education, so whatever our goals were, she would ensure that education was at the heart of it. She also encouraged us to look to further our education. I started with my undergraduate degree and went on to my postgraduate with support from my mum. After that, I went on to develop my career in web development and digital communication.

I would definitely describe my mum as a strict parent, and I guess it is because she had to raise us on her own. I believe she wanted to ensure that we stayed on the straight and narrow and that we became decent individuals. Compared to my friend's parents, my mum was not as lenient as they were, but now being a parent myself, I look back and think that it was a good thing she was that strict. I think I now understand where she was coming from because it could be difficult and I cannot imagine myself bringing up four children on my own. I have just one at the moment, and I find it hard enough even though I have my husband. I believe that if I were in her position, it would be a necessity to be a little bit strict. Although my mum was slightly strict, she still had quite a playful personality within that.

My memories go back to us going on bike rides. We all had bikes, and she would take us to the park where we would go ride bikes together. I also have fond memories of going strawberry picking with my mum and siblings.

My siblings and I are quite artistic in different capacities. Mine, I suppose is drama and acting. My brother Amaechi is a very talented artist. So, my mum took us to weekend classes; me to drama classes and cinema and all the other things that were out there. She made the effort to have fun with us as well as creating those boundaries within the home to ensure that some structure was in place.

We come from a religious background, growing up in the Catholic Church and going to church every Sunday. Evening prayers together as a family is something that she instilled in us which I have carried on to my own family.

As the youngest of the children, I do not think my mum spoilt me. Instead, I think that after so many years in the western world she softened a bit. So, I guess with me being the youngest, as I got older, she was a bit more lenient with me. To be honest, after so many years, I think my mum focuses a lot on all the positives of our childhood; but I think that all of us at different times in our lives caused her some heartache. I can only speak for myself. My childhood, although was filled with great family memories, my school and social life was a blur of peer pressure and bad company. I'm not sure if she knows that I didn't often stay at after school club or netball but found myself hanging with friends in Hackney or sitting in detention. My mum soon realized that something was terribly wrong as I changed from being a very polite and helpful girl to being impolite and becoming someone she did not recognize. She knew that she needed to move me from my first school, Our Lady's Catholic High School. I literally moved overnight to St. Anne's Catholic High School. Things improved greatly and I really progressed and I felt like I had found the good person I thought I had lost. I guess when you have lost someone that early in life, you would want to keep your family close and set up those boundaries to protect your family. For me, it was just motherly instinct, and now that we have grown up, it is clear to see that all through the years, my mum had instilled in us brilliant life lessons that are visible in our personalities. We are all now quite responsible in the family and all thanks to my mum.

The top three attributes that my mum instilled in me has to be determination, belief in myself and selflessness.

My mum taught me that with **determination** there is nothing in this world that you want to achieve that you could not achieve. I got that from my mum without her having to say it. It was just from me seeing what she had gone through and what she has achieved. When I decided I was going to pick up a camera and take some photos and slowly turn that into a business overnight, it was only because of certain things that my mum instilled in me. I remembered her saying, "If you enjoy and are passionate about something and you want to do it, you go ahead and do it." I have applied that throughout my career.

Believing in yourself is linked to determination. Believing in yourself and knowing your worth is a crucial thing because a lot of the time, you may get into a situation where you feel like you are not worthy of achieving something. But understanding and believing that you are worthy helps to arouse your confidence and enable you to stay on track to achieve your goal. Believing in yourself also includes being proud of yourself and your abilities.

The third attribute that my mum instilled in me somehow could be seen all over her, and that is being **selfless**. There were so many times that my mum dropped what she was doing for other people and her family. There is this thing about my mum; she feels other people's pain when things happen. I can see it on her face that she feels their pain and she feels some connection with these people regardless of what they are going through.

My mum is a real community person, and she made me her Mayoress when she was Mayor. So, I followed my mum to some functions and events and then I understood that it was not only about going there, dressed up and being a face. No, it was about going to these events and making yourself available to those people, making yourself open to them as well as understanding what they might need. They might need you to support their community, they might need you to be their voice, or they might require you to be someone that they can lean on. So, you need to be open to them and be there when you are needed. You needed to be that person, twenty-four seven, seven days a week; leaving the house at 6 am and coming back at 8 pm, I definitely looked at my mum and went wow, because it was not an easy thing to do. To be switched on for other people all the time and leaving yourself open requires one to be selfless.

Leaving yourself open for other people to understand your family life, who you are and your background, being open to others shows dedication to the cause of your fellow humans. She was not just that way because she was a Mayor, but generally, that was how she is on her normal day to day life. Sometimes when other people need your help, you need to be aware of that and also be able to concentrate on the things going on in your own life too. You also need to be open to what is happening in other people's lives so you can support them whether community-based or just family and friends based.

Most people think that my mum never worries. I believe that my mum is a wonderful person, but she is not superhuman. I know I definitely do worry. We all worry, but it is how we deal with our emotion that is key. My mum is very good at controlling her emotions, and at that point in time she may be pushing it aside for what is a higher call. If she is in a situation where someone needs her to take charge of a situation; a conference, a talk or speaking to a community, then she knows how to take control of her worry at that moment and suppress it to bring out the confidence in herself. That is one of the qualities of my mum that I admire. I don't think it is an easy thing to do. It is just a part of her. I think it is a quality that is hard to pass down, but it is something I try to emulate whenever I feel nervous.

I believe that wisdom generally comes with age. For my mum, I think her wisdom came from growing up in a village in Nigeria and moving to the town, before getting married and moving to London. Then, with my dad passing away and she not taking any Benefit from the government, being able to raise us with money she earned from her jobs was just incredible. As you can see, all these years of experience I think built my mum's wealth of wisdom. In addition, the challenges that she chose to take on in life added to her wealth of knowledge. It is very easy to get married and come to England and just live; but my mum chose to not only to live, but also to love life. She chose to progress in life to the maximum capacity that God planned for her. As she did that, her wisdom increased. Our wealth of wisdom can only grow when we choose to take on challenges in life coupled with our life experiences just like my mum did.

Being a Mayoress was a lot of responsibility. In the beginning, I did not know what the role entailed, but I learned quite quickly that you were the figure of the community and you were someone who was there to support the community with their needs. You are also someone who should be on hand when any community member or group need support in whatever they are doing; whether it was creating a new organisation to support the community or launching a business within the community that was going to help individuals. So, going with my mum to different functions opened my eyes to what was happening in the community; where help was needed and where the council needed to be influenced for regeneration or to meet specific needs and where there are forgotten groups of the population that need reaching out to. Sometimes, they do not know where or whom to reach out to. It is the role of the Mayor supported by the Mayoress to make sure you are available for such people. You have to be the person they talk to and you try to take some actions to help and support them.

I did not have to take time off work to perform my role as Mayoress because my mum had the Mayoral role full-time for one year. Some of the functions and events are not just during the regular working hours of 9 am -5 pm. Where possible, I attended the evening and weekend functions and activities with my mum.

Anyone who knows my mum very well would know that she is a very organised lady. Especially with my dad passing, she chose her family; family life is very important as well as her career. She instilled in us that having a good career is having a good foundation. So, with my mum, to be honest, I do not understand how she balanced everything. She being a community person did not prevent her from spending time with us, her children and I do not think we felt envious of the time she gave to other people in the community. She spent quality time with us either bike riding as mentioned earlier, going out on trips, checking on our school work and extracurricular activities.

So, she would do activities with us on the weekends, and when it was evening, we would eat, maybe watch TV, mum would retire to her room to do some studying while she was studying Law. All the while she kept working as a fulltime midwife. She would later come in and ensure that we have gone to bed, and do our bedtime routine with us. I am very sure that my mum would be up for a few more hours afterwards doing some work before getting a few hours of sleep and then getting ready for work early the next morning. My mum just coped because that was what my mum does. She is a very family-centred person. Having a career is important, but she brought us up to know that having a close family is very important too.

With my mum, family time was family time. She did not mix family time and community engagement. It was only when we got a bit older and were off to university that my mum actually followed her dream and got into politics. That was when FAWP was formed. When we were younger, although she did a lot of work in the community as a midwife and started her journey into politics by studying Law, weekday evenings and weekends were family time. So, we did not experience anytime where we did not spend quality time with my mum. She even had the time to sit and read books with us.

When I left for the university when my mum made a conscious decision that it was a good time to pursue her love of politics and get into the Council. So, the impact of my mum being more community based leading on to being on the Council and setting up charities etc. were all developed after we had all gone into higher institutions or were all graduated and building our careers.

Of all of my mum's achievements, the one I am most proud of has to be hands down when she became the Mayor of Enfield. If you think of where she has come from and the society we live in, then you would appreciate why that was such a great achievement and why I was so proud of her.

My mum was born and raised in Nigeria before she came to live in the United Kingdom (UK). She coming from a different country and going for such a high political position was not going to be easy. You have to be nominated for a lot of the political posts. In the academic field, it is very easy to say "I am going to study a course" and during exams as long as you have answered all the questions correctly, then you were going to get a superior mark. In politics, however, a lot of it comes down to hard work within the community; being able to communicate with people, being accessible to people and getting on with people and, showing them that you are committed to helping the community. You have to prove yourself for people to accept you before nominating and voting for you. For my mum to have come here and be able to put herself right in the middle of this community to the point of acceptance as someone determined to make a difference, nominated and voted into the role of Mayor, it was indeed a fantastic achievement.

Being a selfless person could obviously expose someone's vulnerabilities which could lead to misunderstanding or some people trying to take advantage of you. My mum has always been someone to stay focused on her end goal, and it had worked for her from the beginning when she started this journey, and that is the way she plans to move forward. I do not think that she has it within her to be a closed book; it is not just her personality.

My mum loves looking after Kamsi, and they both enjoy their time together. She is a very encouraging and playful grandmother. She helps Kamsi develop, and I guess it has to do with all the years she spent being a midwife. I know one of my mum's biggest regrets is not speaking *Igbo* to me and my brother Chukwuma. I think sometimes life just takes over and perhaps she simply forgot to speak her mother tongue. By the time it became a priority, it was very difficult to pick it up. I believe she's making up for that by communicating with Kamsi only in *Igbo* language. It's lovely that at the age of three Kamsi understands more *Igbo* than me and that makes me even more determined to keep learning our wonderful language.

People go through difficulties or challenges at some point in their lives; my mum was no exception. The problem she had was that a lot of the time, there were challenges from different quarters but my mum's principal goal was in bringing us up to the best of her ability. She did not show us signs of difficulties or challenges whether it be financial or otherwise. Looking back now that I am older and know the challenges that adults go through, I know that definitely, my mum would have gone through many especially as she was a widow. I found that my mum was all about making sure that she had a brave face on for her family and I rarely saw her down or upset. Whether or not she broke down behind closed doors is another story, but she never showed us.

My mum never wanted us to feel like we were at a disadvantage because we had one parent. When I was younger and in school, I saw other children with their mums and dads; I knew I did not have a dad, but I did not feel the void because my mum covered both aspects of being a mum and dad. Obviously, it may be different for my elder siblings because they had my dad around for some time, but for me, I had my dad up to age eighteen months, and I can hardly remember anything. We went on all school trips and anything that we needed we got; school uniform and extra things that we needed in school, my mum ensured that we had them. She also paid for extracurricular activities; Ndidi played the flute and took lessons. She was also part of a choir. Amaechi loved art and mum ensured that he got extra lessons. Chukwuma and I took piano lessons. I always struggled with reading and writing, so my mum paid for extra tuition to help me, and she also took the time to do a lot of reading with me to help me improve. To be honest, I didn't look forward to reading with my mum. I think because she wanted us to be high achievers, she sometimes got frustrated when I kept making simple mistakes over and over again. I did really struggle with basic reading and writing. My mum was a bit short tempered with me and this really put me off wanting to develop my reading skills. But I know it came from a place of love as she only wanted the best for us.

At a point, while my mum was still working as a midwife, she set up a nursing agency which ran for some years to help bring in more income. These were the little things that I did not understand back then; what a nursing agency was or what my mum was doing because I was too young to understand. Now that I am an adult with a mortgage, baby and family I understand more about running businesses, and I look back, and I go wow, how did my mum do it? I draw strength from that, and it also encourages me to go ahead and do whatever I want to do. Sometimes, it is a bit scary thinking of how I can bring in extra income, but I believe if my mum could do it, so can I.

My mum is my rock, my best friend apart from my husband. She is someone I look up to. She is someone whom when I have some idea, and I feel like I might not be able to make it work, I think about her. By thinking about how determined she had been, I draw from her experiences, and I feel energised to make it work. Simply put, my mum is my everything.

PROFESSOR KEITH DAVIDSON –Friend

I have known Kate for over thirty years. She and my wife, Blossom worked in the North Middlesex Hospital in the early seventies, and that was how we got to become friends. My wife is currently unwell, hence the reason why I am speaking on behalf of both of us; otherwise, she would have been doing most of the talking.

Kate is an amiable person, there is no doubt about it, and that is why this friendship has lasted so long. She is very caring, and she places other people's wellbeing above hers. She is a person who picked up her political activities and was undoubtedly very committed to the issue of fairness and justice and has worked to make her community better for the good of all.

I did not know her husband, but I know her children because her children and mine grew up together. They visited our home, and we have visited theirs, we all know one another and get on very well. You know some people start as professional colleagues but end up becoming friends and almost sisters; that was the story with Kate and my wife Blossom. You could not separate them. My wife would at times be at Kate's, or Kate would at times be at our place, and they would spend many hours together talking about both their profession and family. They have been on many tours together; European countries, many cruises etc. and they have had a deep relationship over the years. When Kate's relatives come over to England, she brings them over, so we do not just talk friendship, we practised friendship.

Kate has many attributes, and I believe that she has a high set of values that have helped her become successful. Firstly, in terms of her profession, she is a person who believes in dedication and commitment to her work. I am a Professor, and I have seen her dedication and commitment to work. I think that everyone has seen the value of dedication and steadfastness in Kate. She cannot be faulted in that aspect.

In terms of friendship, the value of loyalty to her friends stands out. Another value one would see in Kate is her selfless attitude to life. She puts others first. I think that was what motivated her to become engaged in politics which she believes is to be of service to others and the wider community. I also think in terms of the big picture that she does not only believe in serving others, but also she is committed to the cause of justice and the removal of inequality. Her position in politics is a statement or testimony to the work that she believes in that no boundary should be set for any particular ethnic group in the community. She became a role model in that sense in terms of her political activities when she became the Mayor of Enfield for a year, and before that, she was Deputy Mayor.

At that level, given her background and the community that she is from, she sends a clear message especially to young people that you can aspire, you can achieve, and you can be a leader. She demonstrated leadership, and it is something that could be emulated by others.

Kate has been a source of strength and help to my family especially now with my wife not being well. We have a program package in terms of helping my wife, and she arranged that for us. She is at the forefront of doing good at all times, and we have benefitted from that most recently. In the past, she and my wife worked together, so they supported each other. When my wife needed anything in terms of their profession, she was always there and vice versa. I think they both supported each other in doing another professional program together. Kate went on to study Law while my wife went on to study Social Policy. So, to put it bluntly, in the business of life learning they have been supporting each other in our lifelong learning.

Kate is all for justice and fairness, so if something is wrong, she would be upset, and she would want to do something to make it right. I think if her children were to suffer some unfair treatment or discrimination, she would be annoyed and would go to great lengths to ensure it never happens to them or anyone else again. In politics, maybe seeing somebody being left behind would make her move with determination and with urgency to try and do something about it. In some ways, I think she would be livid against things that could cause certain harm to anyone or things not right morally.

The number one thing that my wife and I learnt from Kate is her sheer determination to look after her family. Her husband died when her children were very young, and she had to support them through education and everything else. She sought out that determination and enterprising spirit within herself. In fact, she is a businesswoman in her own right. I learned that you could succeed with the determination not just in terms of your bread and butter work, but also in building an enterprise that would support you in the long run. You must also learn from her; the spirit of caring and sharing. She has done that with so many people, and she is always willing to share her commitment to education.

There are several of Kate's achievements that I am proud of. Firstly, going back to the basics, the commitment she has shown to my family in good and bad times, and at the moment, it is more of the bad times because my wife is unwell and she has been supporting us without reserve. She has been excellent and has given of herself unconditionally. The second one is the role she played in the local community, especially when she was the Mayor of Enfield. She did not use that ceremonial role to be there, but she used it to make a difference. I think there is a place that was developed for children to play which would be a monument to her term as a Mayor. I am personally proud of her accomplishments as Mayor and to put it bluntly, one of us to occupy that role in Enfield. I am also proud of her achievements educationally because I believe that one must use one's natural intellect to grow and develop and she has done that, and thus she echoes what I believe in.

I see Kate now as a source of influence, passing on her knowledge and experience not just in the community but in the global village. Recently she has been engaging in a number of travels, giving talks and I think the last time, she was in India I believe. So, she has that in front of her as the scope to make her contribution to the broader global village. She has grandchildren too, and she makes time to enjoy their company too. I do not know her other plans, but certainly, she has signalled that she can contribute globally in the fields that she has competence whether professionally or in the broader area of politics and legal issues of inequality and injustice in our world today. I am sure there may be other things she wants to achieve, and I believe she will use her determination and energy to make them become reality.

One thing I must say is; number one Kate is Black, and number two she is female. In this world in which we live, females, especially black ones do not always have it easy in a world mainly dominated by the males in terms of leadership. So, for her being black and female to emerge as an effective, successful leader in our community that is something to be applauded.

BARRISTER JACQUELINE MAZELI –'daughter'

I have known Aunty Kate for about twenty-seven years now, since 1990. She was introduced to me by my mum. My mum and Aunty Kate's cousin had worked together in the Ministry for Information in Nigeria, and when he came to visit Aunty Kate after seeing my mum, my mum introduced me to Aunty Kate and that was that.

After that, we became like surrogate mum and daughter. She looked out for me all the time, and I looked up to her like she was my mum.

I went off to university in Leeds shortly after we met to study and whenever I came home to London during the holidays, I would go to visit her and spend the weekend. We spent time going to concerts together, shopping, parties or go to the cinema. She considered me as her daughter. I know she has four children of her own, but she always referred to me as her first child and her adopted daughter because I was older than her first child. So, that was how I came to look up to Aunty Kate as if she was my mum. She treated me like her own, and through the years, she has looked after me.

When I got married, she attended my wedding. When I had my first child, she helped with the delivery and came to be with me every day. She taught me how to wash him and how to do other things for the baby. She also took on the role of a mother when she did not have to. I made her my son's godmother, and she has been a fabulous godmother.

When she was playing the mother role to me, my mother was still my mother, but Aunty Kate appeared to be more active in that role. She has always been like that, especially when she sees a need. She did not ask questions, she just did what she saw needed to be done and that was what she also did when my son was born.

I knew she was a midwife and I used to ask her questions about what I needed to do with regards to my new baby. She told me what I needed to do in terms of bedtime, bathing, feeding and taking care of myself which was just the sort of advice I needed as a first-time mum and she was there to give it. She has been amazing, and as a godmother to my son, she always remembered birthdays. She always had gifts for him at Christmas and birthdays, and she would also ask about my other child. She is an inspiration, and a parent to all children. She is a single parent with a successful career. She has done well, and she knows I admire her a lot.

At some point, she wondered whether she should do something with her career. I advised her that she should go ahead and study something in addition to what she was doing. She thought she wanted to study Law and she wondered how she would do that while working and I encouraged her to do it. Looking back now, I don't know how she did it, but she did. While she was working, she was also studying part-time and completed her Law degree. She has achieved a tremendous amount really. I think she is just incredible.

I do see some outstanding qualities of her. She is somebody who tries to be fun.. She has very old-fashioned ways in terms of how children should be brought up. She ensured that the children were happy and they did all the social things like going out to family events, seeing friends, going to cinemas, shopping and all those things. So, I do see that fun side of her, and at the same time, I know she has very traditional values.

Some of her traditional values were being respectful to your parents and honesty. I remember being brought up with those values too. I remember always being told when we were young that you do not disrespect your parents, you do not disrespect older people and I encourage my children to adopt these values too. She always attends church with the children and tries to raise them as Christians to have those values and to know right from wrong, so that they would be able to go out into the world and know how to conduct themselves.

For me, I think it is a very valuable lesson to teach children because you are saying to them that this is who we are. We are Christians, and we go to worship in the church on Sundays, so we have to behave like Christians. That means looking out for one another, being loving and living in a Christian manner regardless of whatever else might be going on in our lives. We do not have to say "Oh, I don't feel like it so I won't go," I thought that was an old-fashioned way which is possibly the way she was raised. I admire that she carried that through even though she was working. Being a single parent, you may think that someday she would get tired, but somehow, she always carried on.

I know that she recognised that her children did not have their dad, so she tried very hard to be available and to be accessible to them so that they could feel like they could talk to her. I thought that was very forward thinking for those days - about 27 years ago. So, all through the years I just felt that she was somebody who as a mum, wanted her children to be able to talk to her and be able to say, mum, there is something I would like to speak to you about. I see the relationship that she has with her children and the way that she ensured that when they were growing, they were able to talk to her and find her approachable, especially the youngest, Chinelo because they are very close. It is lovely that she was able to do that. These are the qualities that I see in her, and I find very attractive. I try to emulate and teach them to my children too.

Aunty Kate is also very hard-working. At one point, I remember she was running a nursing agency from her home and at the same time working full time, needless to say, while she was a single parent. She was determined. Some people would have just given up and said , “You know what? I’m doing it all by myself, working nine to five or whatever it is and that’s enough, but I’m doing my best.” She was always pushing herself, doing extra things and she still went into politics. She never really stops. There is this fearlessness, no limits, no ceiling, there is nothing I cannot do, and everything is possible attitude with her. I think that is amazing.

I am most proud of two of her achievements. The first one is her studying Law to become a lawyer but did not manage to take it further to practice as a lawyer because of the difficulty in giving up her midwifery career at the time. This meant that she would have had to fund the new career and give up her old one at a time when she was reaching her retirement. I saw that that was an obstacle. She did do that degree and completed it, and I was very impressed and proud of her for that. The second one I would say would be going into politics and becoming the Mayor of Enfield. I think that was a fantastic achievement, especially as a black woman. I know it is not easy at all to do something like that.

If I could change anything about her, it would be maybe the fact that she is not so easy to see nowadays because she is so busy. We are still close as before, but she appears to be involved in a lot of things now. I don't see her as much as I used to but we are still close, and she is at the end of the phone if I need to reach her.

I am very inspired by her achievements, her dedication, her focus and the way she is very committed to people she cares about. She will do a lot for her loved ones. Some friends in her circle are widowed but more recently, one of her friends lost her husband, and she was there throughout. She visited her friend regularly to ensure that she was okay. She also went to Nigeria with her friend to ensure that she did not have to be on her own when she went for her husband's funeral. That was not an isolated situation, it is just the way she is. If she has a good friend in you, she is a good friend too. That is a wonderful quality that she has.

The biggest thing that I would say Aunty Kate is to me is a surrogate mother because she appears to have filled that role for me. She is someone that I can call unto when I need to speak to a mum, and she would give lovely advice from the heart, and it would be apparent that she is concerned for my welfare and that of my family. She refers to me as her adopted daughter, and it does not feel odd at all because of the way she has been towards me throughout the years.

MRS CECILIA EKE –Friend

I have known Kate for over three decades. I usually call her Kay. I met Kay at North Middlesex Hospital where I worked as a midwifery sister in the labour ward. She was always smart, very kind, industrious, cheerful, polite, and full of empathy and support for her colleagues. She was loved by everybody in the unit and ever since then we became very good friends.

Unfortunately, Kay lost her husband tragically leaving her with four young children. She joggled work with family life and successfully raised all four children academically to degree level. While still working as a midwife, Kate embarked on a part-time course in Law in which she graduated.

After her husband passed away, she coped very well. She knew that she had to bring up the children on her own and there was no way out of it. She pulled herself together very quickly, and I commend her for it because some people would not have been able to do it as quickly as she did.

I don't know how she does it, but she has a way of knowing how much time she has got for certain things, and she never leaves space without filling it up.

She was very interested in politics. She would read the newspapers, listen to the news, etc. She later joined the Enfield Labour Party and soon was elected a Councillor in one of the Wards in Enfield. She performed exceedingly well in that role and then was elevated to the position of Mayor of Enfield. She raised funds tirelessly for various charities for example; Sickle Cell Society, Refuge for battered women as well as mentoring and empowering single mothers on Benefit to get back to education or work.

With regards to Kate's political career, when people know you are friends with someone like her, they will not tell you anything bad about that person because they know you will get angry and rebuke them. So, generally, people, have said that she was a good Councillor and a good Mayor.

She is a motivational speaker, and she is passionate about speaking on various issues relating to empowerment and leadership of women and young people. She advocates that it takes the community in conjunction with parents to raise a child.

She is a good listener. She would listen to whatever you have to say to her and then she would think it over. She will not shout at you as some people would do, but after listening, she would talk to you about whatever you have said.

She is very hard-working; if there is anything that needs to get done, she was on it, even to the simplest of things like carrying chairs. She has a hands-on approach to everything, and she will not say, "Oh, I'm the chairperson, and so I shouldn't be doing such things." She is the type of person who would do anything to make an organisation work.

As one would expect, when she lost her husband, she was concerned about who would be with her children when she wanted to do some night duties? I said to her that I would do day duty and she could bring the children when I am home at night so she could go for her night duty. The children all came in their pyjamas and stayed with me. She would then pick them up the next morning.

Unfortunately, I lost my husband in 2016 after six years of ill health. Kate being a true friend was always around to comfort and support my family and me. She visited us frequently making sure we are eating well, keeping us company, sitting with us and consoling us. Also, Kate accompanied my family and my husband's remains back to Nigeria for the burial. It is also worth mentioning here that Kate volunteered to pay her round-trip fare to Nigeria.

She was also around to offer help when any of my sons were ill. She stayed with me day and night when my husband passed because I was in deep shock. I do not know where she gets her energy from, but honestly, she would pass the night with me with little or no sleep, and the next day she would be up, and you would not even know that she missed her sleep.

When I had to go home to Nigeria with the remains of my husband who was a Chief, she said to me "Cee, don't worry I'll go with you." Not everybody can do that. She not only came with me but also, she insisted on paying her fare. At my husband's funeral when it was time for my hair to be cut, she said she would be the one to do it, and she did it. She completely took over and became my mouthpiece in everything. She made everything easy and straightforward for me because that was who she is. She believes in doing unto others as you would have them do unto you. So, when she is doing things for people you know she genuinely cares, and she does it with love.

Kay uses her time and money visiting the sick, the lonely, the bereaved, and the underprivileged.

This year I have not done anything for her, but the amount of love she has shown to my family and me is more than I can express. I can never thank her enough for it. She supported me when my brother passed away as well. She has done so many things for me over the years and most of them I cannot even remember.

Kate likes dressing up, and she dresses to match. I like it, and she is always smart in her clothes. I think it is all good for her. I usually tell her how nice she looks in her outfits.

Kate is not a quiet person so when I see her sitting quietly for a long time, I think that something is bothering her. I would say to her, "Kay what is it now?" And she would say "What? Oh, nothing." But the thing is, whatever it is, she knows how to deal with it. She does not act on impulse; she thinks over things before doing them.

Kate is a go-getter, and if her son, who is an artist, had followed his mum's advice, he would be a different person today. She wanted the best for him because he is a talented and gifted artist. She wanted him to shine, to be on top of his career. But the boys of these days would always do what they think is right for them even though they know that their parents know better.

Kay has four children, and they are all doing very well with work and whatever they are doing. She gets on well with them. The youngest, Chinelo, was her 'handbag' because before she got married, Kate took her to wherever she went. When we were working at North Middlesex Hospital, Amaechi's paintings and drawings were all over the place. So, by now people would have been paying to go into his gallery, but he seems to be happy with himself doing his own thing now,

She also has a good relationship with her other son Chukwuma who is my godson. Again, the best a mother can do is advice the child, but it is up to the child to take it or not. Didi, her eldest child, does not come home to see her as often as she should, but if there is anything going on such as occasions, she would come. The youngest child, Chinelo, is still her 'handbag'. She has a very good relationship with Chinelo.

Kay also finds time to go swimming. By 7 am, she would be at the pool; about three times a week. She also finds time to do yoga and other exercises to stay fit. I share her passion for swimming. I used to go swimming too.

Kate is a wonderful person. Honestly, she is a one in a million. I have not told her that though. Although, I could have several times because sometimes she does certain things and I would ask her where she finds the time from. She just answered, you make it, and she would continue,

Cee if you want something, you go for it, and you have to sacrifice something for it.

We have maintained our relationship for over three decades even though we have different social lives. Of course, as friends, we have had misunderstandings. Whenever she said something that did not sit well with me, I told her off, and likewise, I would apologise if I had hurt her in any way. For example, there was a time I did something that made her very angry, but I have forgotten what it was now. I remember her brother was visiting from Nigeria that period. I went to her house to apologise.

With regards to her relationship with her husband before he passed away, I believe they had a good relationship. Her husband was on the quiet side, and he was always smiling. He used to accompany her to parties but never got up to dance when she was dancing. He was a lovely man. His passing was sudden and sad for us all.

Kate is involved in so many church and charity, and I don't know how she goes to all those activities, but she is always there. When she told me that she was thinking of studying Law, I said what? How can you think of such a thing with all you have going on? But somehow, she did it.

Kate is an active member of St Edmund's Catholic Church where she is a Eucharistic minister. She is the President of St Edmund's Nigerian Catholics Community, and Coordinator of *Ndinne* Igbo Catholic, UK & Ireland. She is also a member of the Nigerian Chaplaincy Catholic Women Organisation (NCCWO). She is a patron of Congress of Igbo Leaders and also member of International Women of Power. She is also a member of the Advisory Executive Committee Economic Women Forum, and she belongs to so many other organisations that I cannot remember. Kate has won several awards, and I thank God for her, and I am sure she hopes to win more.

MRS BERNICE SARSAH – Friend

My name is Mrs Bernice Sarsah. I currently work as an audit manager for Waltham Forest.

I have known Kate coming up to 22 years now. She is a very helpful person. The first time I met her was when I was sitting in the church and went into labour. She rushed over to see how she could help because as a midwife, it was her area of expertise and she made sure I was okay. From then on, she just kept an eye on my family and me asking how we were doing, and we became good friends. When my daughter, Araba was born, she kind of just adopted her and kept an eye on her. She has been involved ever since; talking and offering advice.

She does a lot in the church, so we bump into each other often doing various things. I have met her children as well. Her children are older than my children, and they went to the same school. It has been good exchanging information.

Aunty Kate was the sponsor of my daughter Araba in her confirmation. It involved praying with her, talking to her and encouraging her. She took her role as a godmother very seriously. Apart from arriving on our doorstep with the presents every year, which she does brilliantly, they also have their relationship. My daughter rings her up and chats with her. Aunty asks about her wellbeing, and she offers her advice and encouragement. For my daughter, it was like having another mum who can offer some advice and guidance.

I am quite close to my daughter, but I am quite happy for her to get opinions of other respectable people like Aunty Kate who has also raised her own two daughters, who are now grown up professionals. They relate well with each other. Their relationship is not like the typical adult and child relationship. There is respect there, but also my daughter laughs and jokes with her like she would with her daughters. They have a very good relationship.

Attributes I love the most about Aunty Kate are first; she is a strong and independent woman. Because of her family's circumstance, she had to work all alone bringing up four children in London which can be very difficult both physically and financially with all the pressures that go with family life in London.

Secondly, she is a spiritual person. She is always in the church. She has a passion for God. She believes strongly in God and that He is directing her life. So, she takes her religion and worship seriously as a driving force in her life.

As a community person, when she worked as a midwife, she worked at our local hospital in North London. Then, she got more involved in the community by becoming a Councillor. I have also met her a few times in the circuit in my old job while working for the council as an executive officer. Also, while working in schools, I met her at numerous evening meetings where she sat as a Governor at some of the schools helping out and giving her input.

When she retired, she became the Mayor of Enfield where she had the opportunity through her high profile, to do more work with women and in the area of health in the Borough. Since she completed that role, she has done various charitable events. She is huge on girl education, and I know back home in her village in Nigeria as well, she has promoted the education of the girl child which is something I am interested in as well. She also does a lot of community work raising funds for her charities.

Aunty Kate has done a lot to influence the community and the people around her. She is somebody who, when you are around her, you know that she is always going to say something positive. She never really sees anything as insurmountable. She likes to work and do her bit to improve any situation. Some people see her as quite forthright and maybe even as aggressive, but that is because of the passion she has for what she does and what she believes and stands for.

I come from a line of strong women; my great grandparents, my grandparents and my mum come from a long line of people brought up by missionaries. We are not from a very wealthy family per se, but we were educated. Education is a huge thing in my family, even going back to my great grandmother who was born in the 1800s in Africa. She was educated. She could read and write in two languages, and that was something that has followed all of us in our family. So, I appreciate other people who are standing up for women who have issues with violence, health care and education; and these are some of the things that Aunty Kate stands for.

Top two things I admire about her are; one, she is willing to stand up and be counted. Two, she is willing to stick her neck out in things that possibly do not concern her but are in areas where she sees she can make a difference. She is willing to go in there if given an opportunity. Also, while doing that, she remains your big sister or your godmother who you can laugh with.

I have been to Aunty Kate's house, and we have sat and chatted about your everyday family things as well. The last time I met her was in church a couple of weeks ago, and she showed me pictures of her grandchildren on her iPad. We have watched her children grow up, and now it is the grandchildren.

I love the fact that she can be who she is. She can be that lady out there who is demanding attention to get things done. She can be the local Councillor who goes and stands in front of everybody despite their race, creed, gender, etc. and say what she needs to say, and she still comes home to be your everyday big sister, aunt and grandma and laugh at things that everyday family laugh at as well. She is adaptable to any circumstance and comfortable at any level with anybody, and she deals with things that need to be dealt with.

To catch her unhappy, there has to be a form of injustice somewhere. Where justice abides, and she is still unhappy, then you know you have delayed her food, and you must produce it at once for her smile to return.

Apart from having her food on time, she loves and enjoys dancing. If there is a party and there is music, Aunty Kate is out there dancing. Dancing makes her happy also does being with her friends and with people who appreciate her.

Amongst her many successes and achievements, I am most proud of her becoming Mayor of Enfield. I think that was really good given her background. It shows that it just was not a flash in the pan. It showed that this was a person of integrity who genuinely had the concerns of the community at heart.

Aunty Kate always showed an interest in my family's life. If I needed anything that she can help with and I ask her, she would help. I think I have been fortunate enough not to have been in that situation. I had gone to her when my daughter was growing up. I took the opportunity to talk to her about what it was really like bringing up a daughter in London and things to watch out for because she had two daughters of her own. I have not been in a position where I had to rely on her for anything specifically. I know she has a great interest in my family and I am very grateful for that.

She is a role model. She is somebody I can think of and say to myself that I can try a little bit harder and put into consideration the difference whatever it is would make on people's lives in the future. She is one of those people whom I think of in those terms. There are a few people in my life like that, and she is one of them. She has done a lot of good for the community, and she is well respected for that.

ARABA SARSAH – Goddaughter

My name is Christiana Louise Sarsah, and my family call me Araba. Aunty Kate is my godmother. I have known her since I was a baby. I see her in church most Sundays. Now I am at the university, I call her every so often to see how she is doing, and she calls me up to see how I am as well.

She is kind to my brothers and me. Every year on Christmas, and on my birthday, even if I have not seen her in a while, there would be a card and a present waiting for me. She would either drop it off or have it posted to me. This is really nice because not everybody makes the effort anymore.

She is always there in any situation if I need to talk to her and I know that I can. A couple of weeks ago, while I was at the university, I called her. I think I was just stressed out and tired. She encouraged me by telling me to keep up the good work and reminded me that I would soon complete my degree. It was good and motivating for me. She was not just my godmother in baptism; she was also my sponsor in confirmation — this involved things like her praying for me which helps.

Top eight attributes I admire about her are one; - she is a powerful lady. I remember going to I think a party in the church hall and one of her daughters mentioned how her husband passed away and how she raised them working as a midwife with all these hours. She went through it all, and it did not feel like it was easy. But she did it all and all those times, she was there smiling. So, I think that is a really good thing that I have learnt from her; to be strong.

Number two, she is very kind. I think she has kind words for everybody. Whoever you are, when you go to her, she always has something nice to say to you that would motivate you a bit for that day. Number three; she is hilarious. She makes me laugh when we talk. It is just the little things she says that I don't think she means to be funny, but they still come out like that.

Number four, she is supportive. For example, during my confirmation, she was there. When she could not attend the confirmation preparation meetings, she would call me to find out how it went, what she missed and how it was going. Number five; she knows how to multitask and everything is done to the best of her ability. Nothing is slacking, and she does everything well even till now that she is retired. I called her the other day, and she told me the list of things she had to do that week and I told her that it was so much. But she never minds doing it.

Number six; she is entirely selfless. I remember she told me that she worked at a Women's Health Centre where she helps out every week and to see how they are. Not a lot of people still care as much about people anymore. She was a midwife, and it is a job I do not think you can do if you are not a good person and you do not care about people. Number seven; she has a beautiful smile. I like her smile. Whenever she smiles, I believe everybody else wants to smile. Number eight; she is sincere. I think if you ever went to her with a problem or in my case with challenges with being a university student, she would say yes, there would be challenges, but you have to keep working at it because nothing comes easy. She is honest in a good way but not like blunt or anything hurtful.

For you to make Aunty Kate angry, you have to hurt somebody else. Not necessarily physically, but if you do something not nice to somebody else, she would feel hurt. I do not think she associates with people who do that kind of thing or bring about that kind of energy. If you hurt somebody close to her, then you will be in trouble because she is quite strong and it takes a lot to hurt her, so if you manage to do that, then I don't know what you could have done. I made her upset once when I lost her phone number and had not called her for a while. She was not very happy when she saw me.

Aunty Kate embraces helping and making other people happy, and I think that makes her happy as well. Also, when people are thankful for what she does, she is happy as well.

Of all of her successes and achievements, the proudest moment for me was when she was made Mayor of Enfield. I thought that was cool because Enfield is not the most diverse area and also with her being a Nigerian woman. When she was Mayor, I used to be in a choir called Children's International Voices of Enfield Choir and the Mayor of Enfield was invited to all our concerts. When she comes, I would tell everyone that she was my godmother and that was really cool.

She always dresses very well, and everything always matches. She is just really kind, and I do not think there are many kind people like her anymore. Apart from being my godmother, she is a good friend and somebody whom if I had any problem, I could go to, and she would be able to help me sort it.

ANDY LOVE – Friend (former MP for Edmonton which is part of Enfield)

I have known Kate Anolue for approximately fifteen years from the Labour Party. I got to know her very well when she became a member of the Enfield Council and we kept in touch. I have come across a lot of her activities in the community.

Now, I would say she is more of a friend because I am no longer an MP and she is no longer a member of the Council which was the formal relationship. She is very busy with all her family and friends and all the work that she is doing in the community, so we do not come across each other daily, but we do meet. She is one of the people whom I got to know through the community, whom I consider to be a friend.

Kate is a very thoughtful person. I think she is very kind. She does a lot of voluntary work that takes a lot of her time. She is very energetic. She organises events regularly which takes a lot of time and energy to undertake. She is also someone who is well established in the community, particularly amongst the Nigerian community and generally, she is a very nice person.

I admire several attributes of Kate. I admire her tenacity. She has taken up quite a lot of what some people would consider being less popular causes particularly the role of women in the community. She has also worked very hard to get the ideas that she believes into a wider audience. I know that it is quite a struggle in doing that but she stuck to her guns as much as she could, and I really admire her. I admire her energy even now, after serving quite a long time on the Council she still does a lot of work in the community. Lots of people would have said, "Well, now is the time to retire gracefully," but she has not done that.

I admire how she has gone about becoming more active in the community and voluntary groups.

We have been of mutual assistance to each other. We organised a number of events over local issues together within the ward that she represented. She was also a good sounding board. If I had an issue and it came up in the community that she was actively involved in, or in her local area, I could sit and talk to her about it. She would explain what was going on and what her role was in addressing the particular issue I was concerned about. I found her very open and very helpful in resolving issues. In the same way, when she came to me whether to do with the Labour party or some community issues or something that has come up in the council, I always tried to get as much time to try and explain to her the perspective I took on that particular issue or concern from an MP's perspective. We have since formed a strong bond of friendship and trust, and I still have great trust in her because I think she is genuinely dedicated to the work that she is doing and has great empathy for the community and the voluntary organisations that she works for.

I think what makes her angry is most definitely when she sees people not doing what she thinks is essential if you are going to work in the community. Things like; people not turning up to events, people not responding to the challenges that we face in the community and people turning their backs on the need that exists locally. These things got to her because she is so dedicated to working in the community and doing things for different voluntary groups. Whenever someone else does not quite match up to the level of the challenges around there, she used to get very annoyed over that, and she would take it up with the people concerned. I know that she had some rough rounds with some of our colleagues in the community just about that very subject.

She has four children and a number of grandchildren, and I think that takes up quite a lot of her time. Another most admirable thing about her is that she has not allowed the needs of her family, which of course comes first for her to get in the way of her other activities. As a result, she is probably busier now than when she was a Councillor. I think what makes her happy is being able to do something in the community that has an impact and gets a response which is not always possible. One of the things in politics, both local and national is you can work very hard on a subject but often do not get much of a response from the people you are hoping to act on behalf of. I think what also makes her very happy is the hard work she undertakes and the response she gets from voluntary groups from the community to the activities that she had undertaken.

I am very proud of all of Kate's work in the community, and it is difficult to pick out one thing. You can only understand Kate by understanding all the activities that she undertakes. I think her being a representative who is on the Council, and then the community for the Nigerian community was very useful. I know Kate has been here for a very long time and a lot of the Nigerian community is relatively new coming into a new environment with a new culture, and that must be very difficult. What she has been able to do is to smooth that path for members of the Nigerian community and the community generally into becoming a treasured local community here in Enfield and to help integrate them and ensure that they receive a fair deal from public services and are recognised for their contributions to the local community. I think she has had a great deal to do with that happening.

To re-emphasise, above everything else, Kate is a very nice person. She is dedicated to what she does. She does not skim on giving time and works very hard at what she believes is essential work in the community. Hopefully again, she will get on the Enfield Council, because I know that she wants to continue to contribute at the council level to her activities and we wish her well for that. Whatever she does, she would be making a contribution to all of the communities in Enfield and working very hard to ensure that they can take over the work that she is doing and help her to ensure greater integration going forward.

BARRISTER CHIEF CHIEDOZIE EZEASOR (*Ichie Ikeoha* of NANKA)-Brother

My sister is a very independent person. She is very hard working. She is deeply religious, coming from a family of deeply religious parents. My sister is also very spiritual and very humane. She can stand on her own at all time. She is an achiever. She is someone who ensures that she achieves every purpose or project she sets her mind to, and she is a loveable person. I can continue to say a lot about her.

She has been an inspiration to me since we were younger until today. She had always played the role of a parent to us especially when we lost our parents. Even when our parents were alive, she was always there to play a role along with our parents. She was like a leading light for the rest of us.

During the Biafran civil war, I was very young, maybe under five years old. I remember she used to cook soup and other foods and she carried them to a market called *Afo Ufuma* in Ufuma town which is in the southern part of our local government area called Orumba. As of today, the market is about a thirty-minute drive, but she walked from our town to the market. She sold her cooked food and buys salt and other items we needed at home and walks back. So, she was a provider for our family during the war despite her relatively young age.

Our father had always been a trader. He was into big transport business and merchandising. He used to go to the present day Cotonou and Chad, neighbouring countries to Nigeria. He bought products and ferried them across to Onitsha and also Jos, where we were. My father used to do that until the onset of the civil war when we went back to our village. That was when my sister started her food business.

She and our cousins walked to *Afo Ufuma*, and sometimes they crossed enemy territories to sell their food. She buys things needed for our family to take care of our parents and us. She was strict, but not so much as to lead to us resenting her. She was outstanding in most things she was doing. She was like a leading model for all of us. We did not have any issues with her. Besides, she left us at a young age.

There was a big birth gap between her and the rest of us, and we always looked up to her. I remember the advice she gave to me when I completed my secondary school. I had always wanted to study Law, but the first admission I got was to study business administration and management in a Polytechnic at Institute of Technology and Management Enugu, as it was then. I said I would not go because I did not want to study anything else except Law. She called me and said a bird in the hand is worth thousands in the bush, and that what a man should never do is to stand still. Also, that whatever comes my way, I should take it and continue moving and eventually it will get to the one that I desire. I took that advice and finished the programme and started working. After a while, I went back to college where I did a Master's degree and at the same time and went back and studied for my Law degree. Today I am a very senior lawyer, thanks to her advice. So, she has been an inspiration to all of us, and that is the kind of thing she does.

She has also helped a lot of other family members by assisting with school fees, etc. and playing some motherly roles especially as a medical professional. Given our background and upbringing, I could not call her by her first name and there was no room for sibling rivalry because she was about eight years older than me.

We did other things together like farming because our father insisted that we all participated in farming. She went to the farm with everyone else despite the fact that she had her food business to run. Our father made it compulsory. Our mother used to take things out for her at our local market. Our father, of course, had a business when we returned to the village. She was part of all that until she left in the early seventies.

When she left, life for our family was difficult because there was no one to shoulder the family responsibility that she carried. There was no assistance from any of us because we were still quite young when she left. I also left to live with my late uncle – my mother's younger brother in Arochukwu – in present day Abia State in the early seventies after she left. I finished my primary school there. I went back to live with my parents and siblings when I was in secondary school.

I have always had a perfect relationship with her as a child and now as an adult. You know she has a strong personality, but sometimes I try to stand my ground. There are things which I would have loved to do some other way and not her way — for example, simple things like getting from the airport to her house in London. I prefer to take a taxi, but she insists on me taking the train to save money; money that is mine. Please don't laugh. Sometimes I try to find a way to circumvent it, but she would always want to show that she was the head.

The other thing she does to show she is the head is when she introduces me to people. She introduces me as her baby brother, and sometimes I give a very serious frown when she says that. Once again, no laughing, please. I do this because some of these people she introduces me to as her baby brother, I am quite older than. I believe that she derives joy in doing that and she will continue. I am used to her introducing me that way, and at the same time, I am used to the same way of resenting it. You know there are some occasions or outings where I would like to feel big and in control and she ends up introducing me as her baby brother, it just spoils things for me. Although, it does not stop me from feeling how I want to feel hence, the reason why I accommodate it in spite of my protests.

All the while we have had a very strong relationship even when she left for the UK. Of all of our family members, I was the first one to visit her in the UK when her late husband was still alive. Incidentally, the day I landed in the UK was the day Prince Charles and Princess Diana wedded on 29th July 1981. I have visited England many more times after that.

Whenever I am travelling out of Nigeria, to the USA or other parts of Europe my sister always insists on me stopping over in England to see her. Especially, when I worked for the Nigerian Government and had to attend trainings and conferences in Europe; I stopped over in England for the six-year duration of the job, and that was every one to two months. She loved it, and she also exploited that because she made me carry heavy food stuff to drop for her. One of her favourites is *Ukwa,* which she loves so much. To show how much she loves it, upon my arrival, the first thing she checks is the quantity of *Ukwa* I brought before asking about my journey.

So, I dropped off her foodstuffs on my way to Europe, and on my way back to Nigeria, I still had to stop over to pick up her clothes or materials, both new and used. New materials would be to make new outfits for her in Nigeria while the used ones would be to give away to relatives and others. She still does that till today.

She was recognised by our community because of her achievements, especially after her Mayoral installation. She was honoured with a chieftaincy title by our traditional ruler as the "*Adajelumba* 1 of Nanka." So, she is an honourable chief in our town.

Last year, I was also elected as cabinet chief, so we also relate in that aspect. We also relate in our local community assistance especially to our village church where she is a prominent supporter. I also try my best in other small philanthropic activities we do together. We keep our relationship strong by speaking on the phone every week. The love we share has transferred to our children and spouses. I was quite close to her late husband, and my wife now is very close to her. My wife also makes out time to visit my sister in England.

We also have similar interests; she likes politics, and I like politics. I have contested elections in Nigeria for State and Federal House, but I was not successful. The difference is that she contested in England and was successful. I studied Law as did she. I have multiple degrees and certificates just like her — we both like academics and leadership.

From the bottom of my heart, I believe most of my sister's achievement was in doing her work as a midwife because she helped bring thousands of babies into this world safely. Because of the home delivery aspect of midwifery that she practised, she was able to touch a lot of lives, and they were able to have a direct and personal relationship with her. That is why that aspect of her achievement gives me more joy.

As for her political achievements, for me, it was like her payday for the works she did during her midwifery days. Now, God is honouring her as the first African to be made Mayor of Enfield twice. It is for this reason that we will be closing down our businesses to be with you all in England this year for her second inauguration as Mayor of Enfield on the 8th of May, 2019. I attended her previous Mayoral inauguration with a few of our community leaders. We expect our traditional ruler to attend this year's inauguration.

My sister assumed the role of our parents and sometimes it is difficult for her to accept that we are grown up and that we could do things for ourselves. Just like your parents still, see you as their child regardless of how old you are. This displeases me sometimes even though she plays that role so naturally and seamlessly.

It is difficult to draw a line between her role as an elder sister and as a parent. It has always been that sister-parent role equally divided in fifty-fifty per cent. Now and then, I take advantage of her role as a parent. If I want a favour from her, I push her to play the role of a parent. Conversely, if I want to feel independent, I push her to play the role of a sister so I can have my way. Generally speaking, I think the situation suits me well. She is a compassionate person and can tell how her decisions impacts on one.

She is an exceptional person with an excellent personality. She is elegant, beautiful and God has helped her to maintain a very healthy living and healthy personality. You would never believe her age. The other night, we went to a party, and people kept calling her my wife. They were shocked when they realised that she is my elder sister.

She worked hard to look and feel the way she does. I know that she has been very conscious of what she eats. She regularly preaches that we are what we eat. As a much-disciplined person, she manages her time very well, and she can do and achieve a lot and still have a lot of reserve energy.

A lot of the time, my sister and my wife gossip about me. Sometimes, I wonder if I am married to my wife, or it is my sister who married my wife because of how much time they spend talking about me. Funny enough, most of the time, my wife uses my phone and phone credit to have these conversations with my sister. That is why I said that the love she has for us has transferred to our spouses. She has a close relationship with my wife, and I believe it is so because my wife is a sociable person.

The other thing that is a little irritating about my sister is that she disturbs me about clothes. She would constantly send me on errands to buy clothes or materials for her. She would have me drop off the materials with her seamstress and pick them up once ready. Apart from buying them from the market and trips to her seamstress, she would also call me to pick up clothes from her friends coming in from Abuja to Lagos or England to Lagos. Once the dresses are ready, I had to find someone to take them back to her in England. Failing that, I have no choice but to send them to her via DHL. I just remembered, she has not refunded me for the cost of the last two packages I sent to her via DHL.

She has always been there for me at all times. During my school days, my father did his best, but it was not enough. Our father was a wealthy man before the civil war, but the war rendered him helpless. He also refused to go back to Jos where he had successful businesses. He was just able to go back there to sell the house he had in partnership with his business associates and restricted himself to the small business and farming in our home town. But it wasn't enough. So, my sister took over the role of being the provider. She supported us financially and funded our education.

There is no major project that my sister has not supported me on. She supported me when I was building my house in the village and recently, she supported me with the completion of my house in Lagos. She also attended most of the major events in my life. When I am visiting England, she makes it comfortable for me. I pray that God continues to give her good health and to prosper her in everything she does. I also pray for God to keep her for us and us for her, and for us to be able to support her as much as she has supported us.

COUNCILLOR NNEKA KEAZOR – Cousin

I have known Kate Anolue who I refer to as my Aunty Kate all my life. She is indeed my mum's cousin. She has been a mentor and coach to me. She was the midwife who delivered my two children; my daughter, Odinakah and my son, Akolisa.

Aunty Kate is a mother. She brings the family together. Every summer, she hosts all her extended family at her place. We know her especially for her spread of different foods. She never asks us to help; all we are asked to do is to show up and eat. It is a fun family time for us, or during Christmas, if she is in the UK. She spends most of her Christmas in our hometown Nanka.

We look at her firstly as a mother figure, not just the adults but also our children. She never forgets anyone's birthday. She would personally deliver our birthday, Christmas and other event's presents and gifts. All our children look up to her, and she is indeed a woman of great value. She has instilled a lot of value in all of our family here in the UK and also back home in Nigeria.

As for when she has been there for me, where do I start? I will share a few with you. First one was during my pregnancy. As mentioned earlier, she was the midwife who delivered my two children, but she was not my midwife during pregnancy. On delivery day, while in pain, I looked up and there she was. She then told my midwife that she would take over from then.

My youngest child, who was delivered over 17 years ago is a day I will never forget. I had him prematurely. I started having pains, and I called Aunty Kate as usual. She told me she was not feeling well and was off sick and at home. She advised me to take a taxi and make my way straight to the hospital. I was unaware that I had great challenges ahead. I was bleeding internally, and I was rushed to the hospital. Upon arriving at the hospital, I was rushed to the theatre and to my amazement there was my Aunty Kate dressed up in her theatre gown already waiting for me. Now, that is a day I will never forget.

When my children perform well in school, and I think who to share it with, Aunty Kate is right there. My daughter is a volunteer for Tender Care Initiative one of Aunty Kate's charities. Recently, while my daughter was in university, Aunty Kate held a domestic violence awareness event. I showed up at the event as a speaker and met my daughter as a volunteer helping out, and I was very proud of her. This is just an example of the type of relationship my children, and I have with Aunty Kate.

With regard to her political life, as a mother to us, we teamed up and campaigned for her when she contested for political office. From 2002 when she became a Councillor for Upper Edmonton & Enfield, I lived in Haringey which was a different Borough, but it did not stop me. She allocated an area within her Borough and gave me leaflets, and I just got on with it and did my campaigning session. For five years, I campaigned for Aunty Kate non-stop.

In 2007, I moved to her Borough of Enfield and turned up to campaign for her. On the day she said to me, "I'm sorry you'll no longer be campaigning for me." I thought to myself that it was a bit harsh, and asked myself, what have I done wrong? She continued by saying that since I now live in Enfield, I will be campaigning for myself. She added that she needed me to go and register, not just as a supporter, but as a member of the Party.

That was a life changer for me. I registered with the Labour Party in 2007 and was made the secretary of the branch on the same night, and that was the start of my political career. The next local election in 2009 I was selected as a candidate. In 2010 I became a Councillor in the Borough of Enfield. As you can see, she has played a fantastic role in my political life, and I also look up to her as my inspiration, mentor and coach. She has also been there for me right from the early days of my political career till date.

She served as the Mayor of Enfield in 2012/13, and she will be Mayor again this year on the 8th of May, 2019. She is currently the Deputy Mayor for the second time, and that is a record in the Borough. I know that the community will celebrate on that day.

As for what drives her, I think first and foremost it is her God. She is very active in her church, and she is a woman of God who would help people notwithstanding the circumstance she finds herself. She does not believe in the word "failure". She is a strong woman, and whoever comes in contact with her, she will work to turn that person to become strong and effective in the community.

Secondly, as a woman, she sees herself and prides in being a woman. She has a passion for women and loves empowering women. She has an initiative called Forum for African, Asian and Caribbean Women in Politics (FAWP). She has the desire to always empower women, and she is doing that. As a retired midwife, she has a passion for women and young women which formed the drive to her other initiatives called Tender Care Initiative. The initiative supports young women who become pregnant in the community by encouraging them that it is not the end of the road and that they can still become successful in whatever they put their mind to.

Thirdly, she also has lots of ideas for young people. She has an initiative called Catch Them Young which encourages and empowers young people to be safe off the street, focus on their education and educating them on politics.

Most people who know Aunty Kate would have heard her life story; her story of being a widow with four young children who as a midwife, went back to the university to study Law. She uses her life story to reach out to people; to tell them it is never over and to tell them it is possible to achieve success.

I am a Biochemist by profession and then went on to gain a Master's Degree in IT Software Design. From being mentored by her and aspiring to be successful like her, I went further to study Law and today, I am a practising solicitor. I give all the credit to my Aunty Kate for her mentorship, encouragement and support.

So, as you can see, she is driven towards making a difference in her community especially the black ethnic minority group, women, young people and all who are disadvantaged in one way or the other; she works hard to provide better services for them.

With regards to her supporting me in my political career, I remember when she asked me to apply to become a Councillor; I said to her that I could not do it because not everyone is like her. I also reminded her that I had two children, and I know she had four, but my two felt like I had ten. I continued that I have a full-time job and I was going through some life challenges. As if I was talking to the wind, she insisted, saying I should go for it.

Anyone close to her would know that she does not give up on people easily. So, I thought to myself that I could not say no to my Aunty. By then I had just completed the application form, but I did not have the drive to send it off. Aunty Kate was monitoring the deadline for application submission, and she kept calling and asking me if I had completed and submitted the form. I had to admit to her that I had completed the form but had not sent it. She then asked for us to look at the form and she was literally on my neck till the form was submitted. On the submission deadline, I believe I may not have submitted the form if it was not for her, because I kept giving her excuses that I was at work and had not had the time to post the form. She then said that the form could actually be submitted via email and she already knows the right email address. By now it was two hours to closing, and with her push, encouragement and support, I finally submitted the form. The rest now is history.

My Aunty Kate has always been there to support from the application till this day. As I progressed from Councillor to Cabinet Member, she was there. Now there are a lot of issues in my role where I am responsible for crime in the Borough, and the Ward she represents in Edmonton is one of the highest crime areas in the Borough, and indeed in London. So, she is also there supporting and guiding me on what is best for the people, what next to do for the people, how best to progress with supporting and bringing better services to Edmonton, etc.

With regards to how resilient she is, I know Aunty Kate has thick skin and can take whatever comes her ways. I have seen her go through a few very difficult times but she always takes things within her stride.

We have similar interests as one would expect since she is my mentor. I am passionate about women, being a woman and having gone through some challenges in life. I also want to show women, especially those of our ethnic group that we can be successful. I am also passionate about young people. As a Councillor, we still have our day jobs. In my day job, I manage transport software and transport for another Local Authority for special needs children. My greatest passion is for young people and those with disability.

I also have a passion for God like Aunty Kate. She attends a Catholic Church while I attend Anglican where I am a Deacon. As for her love for dancing, I enjoy watching her but never would I want to compete with her so I will settle with watching. She is a great dancer, and she is the life of any party that she goes to.

Attending parties is something else she supported me with. When I felt like my role was to be at home with the children and never have time for myself; Aunty Kate taught me that I could prioritise and manage my time. She taught me that outing is not about parents out to have fun whilst their children are left at home. The first thing she taught me with regards to this is how to take my children for outings to have a good time with little or no money spent. So, I took my children to the park for picnics which was Aunty Kate's idea. She used to take her children for picnics all the way to Cambridge, but I never managed to go that far with my children. We also spent some quality time with my children going to the cinemas and outings to community parties. Going to community parties with my children helped them learn about the Igbo culture and enabled them to understand and speak the language. Aunty Kate invites me to these events, and I used to think that I did not have the time, but once I started taking the children along, it became a family outing and that mindset of not having the time was no longer an issue. I tend to attend most functions that Aunty Kate invites me to attend. I said most because I could not match her energy to attend all her invitations. Some of those that I attend, I may make excuses that the location is too far or that I am tired, but then I would think about my Aunty, so full of energy and then change my mind. Sometimes she would offer to pick me just to make sure that she can support me.

With regards to her achievements, there are several of them that I am very proud of. I have been to places because Aunty Kate made it possible. Before I became a Councillor, I had several meetings with the then Member of Parliament for Edmonton, Andy Love. I have also been to the House of Commons when Aunty Kate got awards. I am very pleased that she was the first person who made it possible for me to attend a function at the House of Commons. I was so proud of her when she got several awards at North Middlesex Hospital. The day she had her leaving party at the hospital was when I realised that she had worked for forty years in the same hospital. I could not believe it. When I look at her, I think that she is still ready to go, but she had dedicated forty years of her life to the National Health Service (NHS), that was an achievement that I am very proud of.

In 2012 when she was installed as the Mayor for the first time, my children were her gift bearers. From time to time, when I look at my children's curriculum vitae (CV), I am so proud because they feel so honoured and had to put it on their CV. However, what really impressed me on that day that I had never seen anywhere else, and believe me, I have attended several mayoral inaugurations; was how she invited a lot of traditional rulers from our homeland, Nigeria. On that day, we had the room filled with red-capped chiefs, and we indeed told a story about where she came from and also because she was a chief herself, with the title "*Adajelumba* 1 of Nanka" in Orumba LGA of Anambra State. I believe the same would be repeated on her second inauguration as Mayor on May the 8th, 2019. Enfield chambers will be filled with our traditional rulers because she is passionate about the Igbo culture and tradition. That was a great achievement because that was the first time that the people of Enfield experienced a taste of our culture at a different level. I think it is really important that we showcase some of our traditional culture and heritage, and where we came from. I was really proud of her and how she showcased our traditional culture on that day.

Another great achievement of Aunty Kate that many people are unaware of is that she has got **Honorary Freeman of the Borough** title. She was awarded that several years ago. I think I may be right in saying that she is the first Nigerian, not just Nigerian female, but first Nigerian to be conferred with such a highly esteemed position in Enfield Borough. We are so proud of that achievement. The Nigerian community is proud to have her as a champion in Enfield.

I want to conclude by saying how grateful I am to Aunty Kate because she has not just been a huge inspiration to my life but also on the lives of my children and other young people who look up to her. My son is so proud to have such a person as his godmother. My daughter feels left out and questioned why I did not make Aunty Kate her godmother too. I know that Aunty Kate also treats my daughter as her goddaughter, so she does not lose anything per se.

I am grateful for the influence she has had on my children. She has always been there for them. She knows what school they attend. She knows what they are studying and follows their progress report. And she still remembers their birthday twenty years afterwards. That is really amazing. I don't think I know anyone's date of birth apart from mine and that of my children. I know for Aunty Kate's birthday I would call her daughter, Chinelo to confirm the date that I believe is sometime in March close to the UK Mother's Day celebration. I am very ashamed to admit it.

I am grateful that she is passionate about our community. We need strong women in our community whom women can look up to, and she is one of them. She is in the grass root in the community; everyone in Enfield knows Aunty Kate. It is something to be proud of. She calls me from time to time to inform me of happenings in the community such as people passing away or accidents. She knows everything happening, and she is always out there supporting families in their difficult and most challenging times.

An excellent example of her supporting families during difficult and challenging times happened a couple of years ago. I met a resident of mine in the Ward that I represent, who told me she had immigration problems; no recourse to public funds and other things that follow that situation. She had three children. She complained that she did not have money for sustenance and other things. I was working to see how the council could help her. I asked her how she was surviving meanwhile. She responded that a woman from her church gives her food and other essentials. When I asked her who this lovely woman was, she mentioned Aunty Kate. I could not believe it.

Aunty Kate's car boot is like a supermarket. In there, you will find; super malt, cereals and all sorts of food items. The woman continued by saying that when she meets Aunty Kate at church, she would open her car boot and fetch food items for her. She also told me that Aunty Kate sometimes gives clothes to her children. This is the type of person that Aunty Kate is; it is not just about her immediate family. She has so much in her that she gives to the community. I asked Aunty Kate why she still buys bags of crisps, biscuits and children food after her children have left home. Her response was because she has a lot of children in the community.

Whenever I visit Aunty Kate, I could not leave without her giving me a pack of supermalt to give to my children. I don't drink supermalt, but Aunty Kate initiated my daughter to drinking supermalt. As you can see, she does the same to people in her community, in her church and wherever she meets anyone in need.

Another thing that Aunty Kate is very good is at remembering names. She remembers everyone by their name. I am not that good at remembering names. Sometimes, I tend to rely on her to help me out with names of people that we have met.

I am sure that the entire community in Enfield and London as a whole is grateful for her support. I can never say no to Aunty Kate. If she wakes me up in the middle of the night, I will wonder why she is calling me so late, but I will jump out of bed and be there in a jiffy. If there is anyone else around, they might say that it is late to go out, but I will remind them it was my Aunty Kate calling. I could not fault her. There is nothing she would ask me that I would not do.

An example of this was one time we went to an event and got home in the early hours of the morning. After dropping her off, as soon as I got home, about to get into bed, I got a call from Aunty Kate. She called to tell me that she forgot her mobile phone at the venue. Excuse me I am about to go to bed, I thought to myself. But I jumped out of bed, ready to leave. She knows that I will do anything for her, but also, she is a very considerate person. I told her that I don't mind going back to the venue with her, but I could not drive, if we have to go by taxi or other means, I will go, but I could not keep my eyes open to drive because I was physically drained.

She accepted to drive. I felt bad that I had to make her drive that early hour of the morning, but it had to be so. She drove us there and back. Chinelo, her daughter who lived out of the area could monitor the phone using an app. She tracked the phone while we made our way back to the venue. We were thankful we found the phone at the venue. It was always my pleasure to be able to do anything for my aunty. I am grateful for this opportunity to tell a story about my Aunty from my standpoint. From the bottom of my heart, we love Aunty Kate, and I am so grateful to her.

MRS MERCELLINA (MERCY) ONYEBUCHI - Friend

I have known Kate Anolue for over six decades. We met while in elementary school in Jos, Plateau State in Northern Nigeria, and we have been friends since them. I am not sure how we became friends, but we just did.

As the Biafran civil war was looming, we went to separate Teacher Training Colleges. She went to one in Anambra State, and I went to one in Yola, now the capital city of Adamawa State. During the civil war, we reconnected at Loretta Teachers Training College Adazi, Anambra State. Our friendship is so rooted that our families became friends as well.

Kate got engaged during the war and left to join her husband in London, UK during our final year in College. I was also engaged during the war, but my husband was in the army. Our friendship continued after she left Nigeria.

After my university degree, I had the opportunity to spend a year in a French-speaking country as part of my degree as a French student. I spent the year in France and my holidays; I spent with her and her family. After the year in France, I went back to Jos. Each time Kate is in Nigeria, she visits me.

She never behaved like some friends, whom once they feel they are more comfortable than you; they tend to lose contact with you. Kate was not liked that. She came to visit my family and me. I always looked forward to her visits because she brings lots of goodies for my family and me. We felt her presence anytime she was around. The friendship continued before I moved to America.

When her husband died, I was still in Nigeria. I took an active part at the burial, and I stayed with her till the ceremony was over. When she was given a title in recognition of her performances by their town's chief; I was at the ceremony, where she was installed as *Adajelumba* 1 of Nanka. When her father died, she had a wake. I flew from America to be with her for the wake. When my husband died, she was visiting America at the time. She was the one my brother called to break the news to me. She was there for me and took an active part during the burial.

I believe one of the reasons why our friendship has stayed strong for over sixty years is that we have a lot in common. We also share the same zodiac sign. We have a lot of understanding between us. Even though we have a lot in common, we still have some differences, and I also believe that the differences help tie us together.

She is brilliant, knowledgeable and very hard working. I used to look forward to meeting her while we were in elementary school. She is so talented and very compassionate. She covers for me where I come short. For example, while in elementary school, we had needlework lessons, where we had to sew and knit, and I was not very good at such things. She would step in and do most of the sewing and knitting for me without moaning.

We have never had any misunderstanding. We understand each other very much. If you were to spend time with us, you would laugh till you get tired because we tease one another and tell jokes and say all sorts of funny things and have lots of fun. At times, one might think that some of our jokes are expensive, but it is okay because we understand each other.

There is no major event in her life that I do not attend and vice versa. A few examples; the first time she became Mayor, I was there at her inauguration. Last June 2018, during Adaure Igbo Women Association UK & Ireland inauguration where she is first Vice President, I was there at the event. Early this year 2019, my brother in Dallas who is a priest celebrated his 25th anniversary as a priest, she was there at the event in my hometown Nimo, Anambra State with her sister-in-law and her brothers. I was not there, but she represented me fully. In May this year, she will be installed as Mayor for the second time, and I will be in England by God's grace for the event. My ticket is already booked.

She has always been there for me through life's challenges too. For some reason, I am not sure if it was by coincidence or fate, it seems that we experience similar life challenges. If it happens to her, soon it would be my turn. Few examples are; when her father died, I lost someone in my family, but it happened after a few years. When her mum passed away in 2018, I was terrified because my dad was very sick and my mum too at that time. I kept in contact with her but also at the back of my mind, I kept wondering what was going to happen. And lo and behold, within two months my dad passed away. Similar 'coincidence' happens in good things in our lives as well. For example, if I have a baby today, she will have hers the next day or a few days afterwards. It seems like our lives have been planned somehow, but I cannot explain.

She is very sociable and loves to dance. I love dancing too. But I think she dances more than me. Here in Dallas where I live, some people do not know my name; they only know me as the lady who loves to dance. I love dancing, and I love keeping up with the latest dance moves because I visit Nigeria regularly. As for having a dance-off with her later this year during her celebration of life, I will not bother because I know she will beat me hands down. Why? Because she exercises regularly and she stays very fit. She frowns at me putting on weight and not exercising regularly. So, there is no competition.

She is very energetic and puts in a lot especially for the Igbo community. She is the patron of some Igbo communities, coordinator or chairperson of others, and she is very active in all of them. She loves everything Igbo. She is also very active in her church community where she was president of the Christian Mothers in her church. She also likes to empower the youths especially the black minorities. She gives talks around the world. Last year she was in India and Nigeria for a women's conference. She has travelled far and wide; she has also been to Turkey and gone on cruises. She balances her life; politically, socially, spiritually and family of course. One wonders where she gets her energy from.

June 2018, I was in London for the inauguration of Adaure Igbo Women Association that she was the first Vice President. After a very long day and night, she made sure we went to church the next day for 9 am, or 10 am Mass. She also cooked some food to take to a meeting she had after Mass before we left to the church. She had many people asking her how to get into politics, and she told them that they have to start from the grass root. She is an all-rounder, and she excels me in that. I like to get involved, but not on the scale that she does.

There is something about her that still puzzles me. You know that she is very sociable but at the same time she is very meticulous and I don't understand how she can be so. There is no halfway for her, everything has to be perfect, and we differ in that aspect also. She is also very clean and tidy. One would assume that someone who is very outgoing, who is very involved in things and very sociable may have some flaws. But on the contrary, she is very careful with what she says. I have never seen her do something that necessitated an apology.

What irritates me about her is that she wants things to be well organised the way they are. If you go to her living room, you would think no one has sat there for ages. You go to her kitchen everything is perfectly in place as if they do not get used. On her floor, you will not see any dirt. I am just not wired that way.

The reason why I get irritated is not because of how her things are but because I know what happens when I am visiting her. I try and keep up with her tidiness and 'perfect' structures for a few days and then I am back to my old self. Then she starts moaning. When she starts whining, I simply remind her that I am on vacation and it is not my place to keep putting things back the way they were. I also remind her that when she comes to visit me in Dallas, I do things for her.

The truth is, even when visits me in Dallas, instead of me playing the host, she ends up playing the host. Often, I would call her and order what I would like her to prepare for me to eat. She would moan that I am not acknowledging the fact that she is my guest. I will then tell her that I am expecting my meal at a particular time or else I would not eat it. She will end up preparing the meal for us to eat. She is just so nice. It is really fun to have her around. I would also boss her around and send her on errands. I would tease her and tell her that she has to do the errands even though she is the Mayor; she has no jurisdiction in Dallas. When I am visiting her in London, she gets back at me. She plays host, but she bosses me around.

As for my proudest moment of her, it would be when she was conferred with the chieftaincy title of *Adajelumba Tulugo1* of Nanka by their town's Igwe and also when she became Mayor of Enfield. Her chieftaincy title means - the daughter who excelled in a foreign land - and it was well deserved. As you know, it is hard to for black people especially black women to penetrate the white-dominated society. So, for her, as an African from Nanka, working so hard to be made Councillor and then Mayor; she is really worth it. It amazes me that she could achieve so much in a foreign country where the bar is set so high. For these reasons, I am so proud of her.

You know her husband died at a young age. Luckily, she was already a professional midwife. One day, she called me and said that she was now a lawyer. I was shocked because she never mentioned that she was thinking of applying to become one let alone studying to becoming one.

I have never heard her say she is tired. Most times, she calls me at 1 am, or 2 am UK time. When I ask why she is not asleep, she would respond by saying that she has too many emails to respond to. And guess what; sometimes she would still call me at 5 am, or 6 am the same day. I would be wondering when she sleeps. She is just incredible. I think God gave her the strength of two or three people.

The other thing we have in common is fashion. She likes to spend money, I also like spending money. Sometimes when she visits, we go shopping. The three words I would describe her with are; honest, hardworking and compassionate. I wish everybody had a friend like her. I would not want to change anything about her. Being meticulous is not a vice per se because she would not be a perfectionist otherwise. I believe her being meticulous is not about being cruel; rather, it is what helps her stay organised. It is easy and effortless being friends with Kate. We did not make any effort to be friends, things flowed naturally between us. People love being around us because we make them laugh until their sides ache.

Surprise, surprise! I found out only recently from my mother that she named my younger sister Kate after my friend Kate. My mother told me that because I always talked about my friend, she grew fond of the name and named my sister after her. I told my friend Kate this just this year. I teased her by saying that if only my mother knew how bad she was, my mother would not have named my younger sister after her. She just laughed and said I was crazy.

Some of our children have met. When she was installed with her chieftaincy title, I travelled to her home town with two of my children, and they met her children who were there with her at the time. I wish everyone had a friend like Kate. Like the saying goes over here, "Don't look for a good friend, be a good friend yourself." Our friendship is infectious. We are friends with one another's friends too. Sometimes I tease her by saying that all those years in elementary school, I never knew I was dealing with a future Mayor. I love her very much, and I pray to God that our friendship continues until we are no longer here.

MRS VICTORIA AKUBIKE – Friend

I have known Kate since 1984, which is 35 years. We met during the birth of my second son at Whittington Hospital, where she was the midwife in charge. We became friends soon afterwards. Kate is such a wonderful lady. She motivates people. She is helpful and a good listener. She tries to help everyone whenever she can. These qualities attracted me to her.

What I most admire most about her is that she is a very hard working lady. When she sets any goal in life, she works toward achieving it, and she usually achieves it. I am very proud of her achievements. Firstly, she was a midwife for over 40 years, and she made a huge impact on people's life in North London. Secondly, when she got very active with community work, she became a Councillor because of her hard work. Thirdly, she progressed from being a Councillor to Deputy Mayor and then Mayor. These are great achievements that require hard work for one to achieve.

She is also a woman of the Borough; meaning that irrespective of where one is from, Kate is ready to help and she is ready to push herself to help you. Whenever you need her, she will be there for you. She was there for my children and me when my husband travelled to Nigeria and had an accident. She was also there for me both when my husband and my mum passed away.

When Kate lost her husband, the children were very young. She raised all four of them single-handedly. I was there for her and her children. Then the children were in St. Edmund's Catholic Primary School which was behind where I lived at the time. At the end of a school day, her children would walk round to my place and stay with me until Kate returns from work. When our children were young, we used to attend parties together with our children. We visited one another's homes where we shared meals and laughter. It was quite a wonderful time we had. We still have wonderful times together after the children have all grown. Because of the love I have for her and how much I admire her, I made her the godmother of two of my children; my second son and my only daughter.

Kate loves fashion, and she is a fashionable lady. I admire her figure. She exercises regularly to maintain her figure so she could continue to wear stylish clothes. She loves dancing too. We used to be dancing partners. Fashion and dancing are what we have in common.

Kate is a woman not just for the black community, but for all communities. A lot of people from different communities visit my fashion and beauty shop in Edmonton High Street, and they all speak well about her. They speak of how she helps people during challenging and difficult times. Most of the time, you will find someone who would have something negative to say about someone else. But with Kate, it is different. From my standpoint and from what I have seen and heard, I like to believe that 90-95% of both men and women in Edmonton like Kate.

JENNY CHIKA OKAFOR - Friend

I have known Aunty Kate for about 30 years now. I met her through a mutual friend. Aunty Kate is an extraordinary human being. I struggle to find words to describe her. She is loving, kind, honest, caring, dependable and above all, trustworthy. She is the type of person you can trust with your life and go to sleep without worries.

She hates injustice and will always stand up and speak against injustice against anyone no matter the person's background, religion or gender. She believes in equality for all and in giving. She is lovingly called Aunty or Sister Kate. These are well-earned titles. She is indeed a mother and an Aunty for all, and she is very well loved and respected within our community. What I like the most about her is her outstanding honesty, trustworthiness, loving kindness and above all, her belief in herself and her ability to fearlessly go for whatever she wants. Oh, how can I forget her charitable works and sense of giving?

There is nothing about Aunty Kate that I do not like. No one is perfect, but in my world, she is perfect. She has helped to shape the person that I am today, and I am very, very grateful to her. Oh, the only thing that may have irritated me about her is being dragged along to events where she would then dance better than everyone leaving me "madam left leg dancer" to struggle to meet up. She is a great dancer.

I am very proud of all her achievements. She is a woman, who like many others found herself a widow at a very young age. Despite the challenges, she defied the odds and raised four amazing, high achieving children. While raising these children, she held down her job as a nurse, ran a nursing agency, went back to university and bagged a Law degree. There is also her adventure into politics which has led to her being the first black Mayor of Nigerian origin in Enfield. That was record breaking, and she is set to break yet another record by becoming a Mayor twice. Being a politician who is always under public scrutiny is tough, but she has paddled her political career gallantly and without any scandal. That is admirable.

I always relied on Aunty Kate for guidance and emotional support. I am naturally a very vibrant but extremely soulful and sensitive person. Many people do not know it, but I hurt very quickly. When I do, I recoil into my shell, and this can get serious to the point of depression. However, braving it and talking to Aunty makes the load light. She brings sunshine and light to dark times. She holds your hands and lovingly guides and supports you all the way through.

I have had many tough times, but she always stood by me and never judged me. My pains just like everyone else's pains are always hers, and she will never forget to offer solutions and help to see them through. I am most grateful to her for being the sister I never had. She sometimes forgets that some of us have to be allowed to carry our burdens alone so that we can learn, but that is her overwhelming loving kindness which I cherish like life. She is simply amazing.

Aunty Kate is a very strong woman but also like every woman, she has her emotions and doubts too. Nevertheless, her responsibility to herself and others stands out and helps her to get through difficult moments. As a result, she always paddles through, standing tough and strong. She is a typical woman who will never let you see her pains but whenever occasion demands, a few kind words and encouragement have helped, and we have always held hands and supported each other. I selfishly always look up to her for moral and emotional support no matter the circumstance.

We have shared many fond fun memories. We have danced and laughed together in her home and parties. I love to eat good, healthy diets and can cook but won't cook. So, like a typical greedy person, I always look forward to being fed by her. She is a fantastic cook, and you will never leave her house without being fed and taking food packages for after. Every moment with Aunty Kate is memorable, but the most memorable was dancing with her at her second daughter's wedding. It was a wedding and a half, one of the best that year. She looked amazing and very happy. I will never forget that day.

Aunty Kate should be a friend, but she stopped being a friend a long time ago. She is family to me, and I love her very dearly. My children have on a few occasions threatened to report me to Aunty Kate because they believe that I listen to her. She always weighs in to find solutions to some family issues where I go on a rampage and refuse to budge. I am a very determined woman who can sometimes be inflexible. I am most pleased that I have Aunty Kate in my life. She is very special to me and many in our community. We look up to her to draw great strengths. I am pleased to be her crazy friend and sister who she has to put up with forever and for always.

Imagination is the beginning of creation. You imagine what you desire, you will what you imagine and at last you create what you will.

\- **George Bernard Shaw**

Epilogue

Wow! It has been a long journey for me, coming from a small town called Nanka in Orumba North Local Government, Anambra State, Nigeria to where I am today. Nanka, a town I am so proud to come from, has a population of over 40,000, very industrious and hardworking people; and this is where my drive comes from. I have enormous stamina, and I am a very disciplined person. This is just one of the qualities of a true "Nankarian." Despite having the worst cases of erosion in Anambra State, the Nankarians hearts are not dampened. We never give up.

Education is the greatest asset in Nanka and its community, and those who can, always assist in the funding of education of the less privileged. This is the strength of the Community. The first person from Nanka who travelled overseas to study Management was as far back as 1903. This was gradually followed by other Nankarians who went abroad to study Medicine, Political Science, Engineering, Mathematics, Banking, and the list goes on. Today, that small town Nanka can boast of many Professors, Engineers, Medical and Veterinary doctors, Top Public Servants, Pharmacists, Bankers, Accountants, Top Politicians, Mega-Entrepreneurs, wealthy businessmen and women and so many more. Thousands of Nankarians are now in the diaspora.

In this book, it appears I have poured out my mind by narrating my journey since I left Nanka, but I don't think I have accomplished my desired thought up to this grand age. I feel everyone should have an opportunity to look back into their past; there are lessons to learn from others and also some from me. First and foremost, getting a good start in life should not be a privilege for some; it is every child's right and all children deserve the best possible start in life. My father gave me that good start, and that has helped me to build into the person I am today, of which I am most grateful.

We all have visions for our children, and we seek ways to develop strategies to meet our aspiration of raising world-class children. High quality, early education, childcare and getting it right are central to a parent's visions, and also the opportunity to expand the child's mind. People always ask me how I managed as a single parent to bring up four children. When I look back at the hurdles, I, first of all, remind myself that children are a special gift from the Almighty and one thing parents want is to make sure that they give their children the best. I hold my father with high esteem for that.

I feel there is no set rule designed for parents to follow in bringing up their children. Nevertheless, there are essential points parents need to bear in mind that will help their children to develop and thrive without overpowering them. At times, it is difficult to realise when you have overdone it, especially when we think of the traditional way we were brought up and we feel we know better. In some aspects it is fine, however, in this twenty-first century, the method of doing things have changed immensely. We cannot cocoon our children any more than they will accept from us. Most of the unconscious parenting strategies can go wrong due to the way we impose our ideas on our children. The relationship could be strained and may involve external bodies like Social Services, and even the child wanting to move out of the family home, and they could end up in bad company. When we parent consciously, we develop the habit of being a parent as well as a friend to our children.

By so doing, you would be more in sync with the spirit of your children, enabling you to achieve calmness. Thus, you build lasting trust and a better relationship with your children. I found myself more relaxed with my children, and I could feel that aura of peace in the household which helped me so much. I was then able to cope without much stress. I also have my brothers and trusting male friends who helped advise the boys. It takes a village to raise a child, and I still believe in that wise saying.

Teachers are the second most important people in our children's life, yet some parents do not realise how important it is to work in partnership with the school. Parents are teacher's partners, and our children will benefit more when both work together as a team to support and guide their progress. Positive parent and teacher relationships make children feel good about school and will help them to succeed, knowing that the two important people in their lives are working together. This partnership helps to recognise problems when it arises and ensures that fast solution is provided.

It was not easy for me; being a mother and father could be stressful at times. There was no male role model in the house, but I was not discouraged. Bereavement, single parenthood and loneliness, especially when the children have grown and left home could have been a big issue for me. But it was not because of my involvement in many voluntary organisations in my Borough which is Enfield and also the church where I worship. Being very active and getting involved in the community is a win-win-win for me, the church and the community. Helping out in women groups and youth centres kept me busy. It was a good way to meet lots of people from the diverse community, make friends and build a good support network. There is no need of staying indoors and feeling sorry for yourself; go out and be empowered, be motivated by the amazing people you will come across through your networking. Be warned and be prepared as not everybody you come across would like you or like what you are doing. Do not look back, be focused and take criticisms with pride, but NEVER be a follower. I have met a lot of antagonistic women, but at my age, I am a much wiser woman who can handle anything with dignity. I am blessed.

I came to the United Kingdom to join my husband, and as soon as I qualified as a nurse, I visited Nigeria with my Nursing Certificates to show my dad, and this made him proud. When I left Nigeria, I had a strong belief that I will be back to my country a wiser and more knowledgeable person. Never in my wildest dream did I envisage that I will spend forty years working in the National Health Service and also spend all the good qualities of my life in the UK. And neither did I ever dream of being a politician. In fairness, I have no regrets, because I made the most of the time I spent in the UK. Knowing that I assisted many women in bringing their babies into the world, gives me a lot of joy. I spent over ten years in the Local Government, and being the Mayor of Enfield 2012/2013 is an experience that will remain with me all my life. I learnt more of Enfield and the community, having lived in the Borough for over forty years. I was empowered by many people in different categories whom I met at work and in the community.

Never say never and don't let age be a barrier to your dream. As long as one is alive, nothing can stop you from trying to fulfil your dream, but yourself. When I left the Council in 2014, I believed that was the end of that era, but you know what, never, say never. That is what I said when I found myself back on the Council in 2018; and to crown it all, I secured the highest vote to be the Mayor of Enfield for the second time. Wow, that is amazing and exciting for me

The FIRST NIGERIAN FEMALE 'DOUBLE' MAYOR in the UK. This opportunity is a wakeup call for me to do something different for Enfield. Immediately, I put on my thinking cap and visited a Borough that has Young Mayor. I was intrigued after learning so much about the outline of the Young Mayor's duty, and I wanted to introduce it in Enfield; something that can make a difference in the height of youth crime in the Borough. I was over the moon when the Leader of Council said it was a good idea, and a meeting was held with the Law & Governance Officer, the Leader and Chief Executive of Enfield Council, and the green light was given.

There are so many opportunities in the United Kingdom, and as an ambitious Nankarian, I had to make the most of it. This was when I thought to myself, I have fulfilled my father's request by training as a Nurse; I must get myself into a University to study Law. I was brought up in a typical traditional way that is "unconscious parenting". In those days, children must be seen and not heard, and I had no say or choice in my career pathway. My father wanted me to be a Nurse, and as far as he was concerned, it is good for me, and that was it. We believed that everything our parents say is fine and even if it is not, who are you to challenge your parents.

There is nothing wrong with adult education, majority of people from developing countries reach their academic desire in their adult life. This is because it is less expensive studying part-time and one could equally manage his or her job either full or part-time while studying at the same time. The beautiful thing about adult education especially where there are children is that the adult student becomes a perfect role model for the children. As a professional, my children wondered why I was studying again; after all, I am a midwife. My explanation is that I have a mission and will not stop until it is achieved. There is no age limit for studying; motivation and determination is the way forward. Do not ever allow anyone to tell you otherwise.

Sometimes our imaginative and creative personalities are stifled by our fears and inhibitions. I believe in self-reliance. I am sure of myself and proud of whom I am with humility. Those who garner the most respect are those who are proud of their individuality. In doing this, you can never disappoint yourself. My philosophy of life is to work hard and impact on people's lives particularly women and young people. I believe in honesty, sincerity, and uprightness; however, no human is 100% perfect, but one must try to be above average.

It saddens me that in this twenty-first century, there are still many developing countries where girls are denied education and continued to be treated as second class citizens. There should be access for all girls and on equal levels with the boys. Knowledge is power and wealth, and it is definitely a positive route to get away from poverty. I have always believed that my success in bringing up four children single-handed was not only because of whom I am but because I had the education, then employment, hence I was able to provide for my four children without recourse to Social Services. I also did not rely on nine to five jobs; I worked extra, like agency nursing to supplement my salary, as I had a mortgage to pay. I had little investments here and there. Whilst I was caring for my young family, I was at the same time thinking of my retirement. I did not want to be a burden to my children, at the same time; I wanted to maintain a fair standard of living in my retirement.

I have received so many awards including honorary doctorate for Global Leadership from Academy of Universal Global Peace (AUGP) USA for which I am most grateful, but my greatest award is from the Almighty, and that is good health; for I believe that health is wealth. This is what gives me joy every single day as I wake up.

I believe that whatever we want in life, we must plan and never give up even when we fail the first time. "Life is like photography; you need the negative to develop."

WHEN YOU UPLIFT A WOMAN, YOU UPLIFT A NATION, AND WHEN YOU EDUCATE ONE WOMAN, YOU EDUCATE THE WHOLE WORLD.

We delight in the beauty of the butterfly,
but rarely admit the changes it has gone
through to achieve that beauty.

– Maya Angelou

About The Author

Kate Anolue served as Mayor of Enfield, England from 2012 to 2013. She is serving as Mayor of the same Ward again from 2019 to 2020, making her the first person from the black ethnic minority to be 'double' Mayor. Kate Anolue worked as a midwife at North Middlesex Hospital, London for forty years. Her work in the community exposed her to the opportunity of working with vulnerable women and young people. This ignited her enduring passion to add value to others, which led to her interest in politics. She became a Councillor, which then led to her role as Deputy and then Mayor in 2012.

She has founded Tender Care Health Initiatives, a non-profit community interest company & Forum For African, African-Caribbean And Asian Women In Politics (FAWP) and supports various charities and organization that promote women and youth empowerment.

Kate Anolue lives in England, UK and would love to be remembered as the lady who loves to dance.

'Double' Mayor, Kate Anolue

The new Chief showing off